Shards

a life in pieces

The unexamined life is not worth living.

Plato, attributed to Socrates

Tuna Cole

Cover concept by Tuna Cole
Front cover photos by Doug Tracy
Back cover photo by Mikiko Cole

Shards, a life in pieces
Tuna Cole
Original Copyright 2010
Revised Edition Copyright 2014
ISBN: 978-0-9855702-1-7

Keywords: humanist philosophy, identity, social theory, religion, environment, poetry, polemics

Second edition printing: August 2014

__Dedication__

I dedicate this scatter-gun collection of *pensees*, of suspended dialogues, to my children, Petra, Ariel, and Loren, who over months and years inspired the better part.

Tsumaranai mono desu. Gomenasai.

Foreword

Why shards?

What I offer here are fragments, artifacts. Randomly shaped, ragged-edged chunks of what once was a whole vessel. Or not. Hell, this entity may have been cracked and missing pieces for decades. Some of the chunks seem to fit together; others are quite diverse in terms of color, affective contour, or tone. But even resigning ourselves to never being able to put Humpty Dumpty back together again, perhaps these pieces will give us hints, glimpses of this ol' boy in various contexts. And maybe that's enough. We're all constantly changing anyway— shedding a piece here, adding some contour or depth there; like a snake growing out of its own skin, sloughing off no longer functional segments, adopting different positions/shapes/outlooks toward evolving conditions. Growing.

If there is no fixed, discrete, holographic image to capture, if the Whole Event can never be wholly documented— lacking, through our mutable/fallible humanness, the Eye of God—then these interpretations, or your own, are what we get instead.

My Webster's New Universal Unabridged Whiz-Bang Dictionary (1983) accounts the word *shard* thusly: *n.* [A.S. *sceard,* from *scearan,* to shear, separate.]

1) a piece or fragment of an earthen vessel, or of any brittle substance; a potsherd.
2) the shell of an egg or a snail; a scale.
3) the thin, hard wing cover of a beetle or weevil.
4) a gap, as a gap in a fence; an opening in a wood. [Obs.]
5) chard. [Obs.]

6) a boundary or division. [Obs.]
7) dung. [Obs.]

I suppose I'd pretty much sought the general sense of meaning #1, but *any brittle substance* sent me off on a mental arc in which my skull became the rigid, fragile material cradling simmering thoughts in the febrile stew of my cerebrum. Subject to cracking into pieces easier than I'd care to contemplate.

Most of the other definitions were unfamiliar but plausible. Ah, but having *dung* (albeit obsolete) as an alternate meaning is truly serendipitous! In all likelihood, many of these glimpses will be seen as essentially one form or another of large mammal excrescence, anyway. It's gratifying to know there is etymological precedent.

The question, politely skirted 'til now, is *Why should anyone care?* Even if these shards accomplish the goal of giving the reader a fractured composite of this oily Tuna, what's that to your average citizen, who is apt to have her/his own private struggle in keeping the pieces from falling apart? It's that ol' dilemma: I am you, and not you. In so many ways we share aspects of the human experience; so much overlaps. Conversely, to be sure we are often at odds, occupying profoundly different positions. Because of our common humanity, I accept that you have things to teach me—though the means of that occurring is not yet clear. Do I have things to teach you? Which is to say, are you teachable, and are you open to learning? My hope is the reader will slide in, among, under—all those locative prepositions—around, over, and through these scattered artifacts (*Watch out! Don't cut yourself; some of the pieces are sharp!*), encountering strange and curious beings in some instances, familiar presences in others.

This second edition contains several new chunks, as much as a third more poetry and prose, in addition to boosting the voltage *and* horsepower of several pieces published in the first round. I keep discovering new episodes that cast more light on this unique *and* commonplace being.

Rest assured, there is precedent for revisions. The venerable Walt Whitman, finicky to the end, published no less than six editions of *Leaves of Grass*. Finally, the whole of the text has been rearranged and reorganized, that is to say, rejiggered, in hopes of making it more accessible and appealing.

Tuna Cole
Portland, Oregon
August 2014

Acknowledgments

Burt Jurgens was especially helpful in the initial incarnation, as well as this edition. Furthermore, I received organizational help and advice from Sione Aeschliman, and formatting/layout assistance from Aaron Simon and Bradley Whitaker. My deep thanks to you all.

My three children have been the primary sources of inspiration for these fragments, but others have been legion. The usual confidants, especially in the run up to the first edition, were my fellow Small River pilgrims—Genrul, Dogless, Jambles, Quarrel and Phip. They were sounding boards for many of these works, whose responses typically ranged from befuddlement to incredulity, to out-right derision, to catatonic trance.

I, of course, recognized their reactions as a clumsily thrown-together ruse; I took their crude objections to this or that text, their halting, inchoate resistance, as tough-love *encouragement*. Do you suppose I read their disparaging 'encouragements' wrong? That my marginally coherent, questionably significant observations were best kept hidden in a brown shopping bag in the back of the closet, to be unveiled at such time as the society had sufficiently evolved to be receptive to the themes expressed? Or even later!

Too late now.

Contents

Part One

Grackle's cadenza	15
Personal disavowals	24
Letter to the President	25
Long hair and the art of disabusing first impressions: on choosing the fringe	30
Identities: *Who'dja say you were, again?*	33
Alpha/not alpha	36
Paterfamilias buffoonius: a projection	37
Inferences about the dominant narrative	40
Not just being, but me	45
The effective, affective element in discourse	46
Intelligent design? an apostasy	49
We know very little	53
Faith: meanings, applications and consequences	54
Mir Ghat	59
Two questions	61
Dark clots in the atrium: a sorta gothic tale of (near) woe	62
Logos	68
Sunday in the park	71
I get asked	73

Part Two

The media according to Grackle   77
Ketchup (Impatience)   88
2005, the Golden Anniversary of rock and roll   89
Toward a secular ethic   99
God in one   101
Allegiance: a hierarchy of identities   102
The *other* Vietnam War   106
Not sown   111
Time travel: the mind is a dangerous thing   112
Gnawing evening   115
Dialogue with the Devil   117
In the beginning   129
A modest proposal   130
Waiting   133
A bookstore coffee shop, an interpretation   134

Part Three

Grackle and the environment   139
Stewardship   152
Which is the way   156
On being presentable   158
The environment   159
Paean to Mt. Tabor: the commons   161
Overpopulation   162
On false dichotomies: us vs. them   164
Carlos, the magician   167
Druid working papers   168
In pursuit of harmony: Galen's theology   173

With seeming ease   172
The question of belief   176
Apples/oranges department: observations
          on perceived dichotomies   180
From a letter to an old friend   187
Titles   189
The commons   190
Green terrorists   193
Departures without arrival   198
On giving   199

Part Four

Grackle's thorn: Hercules Aphid   203
Opacity   212
Too much/not enough   214
Intent on finding   215
Voluntary solitary   216
Civic accountability: an employment application   219
We all grew up   221
A good burn: the scream of salmonberry   222
Cosmic justice   226
Milestones   234
Tuna and the three bears   235
Moral value ethics   245
The sole constant   248
Pip's *Kanreki*   250
The rooster, imperiled   254
Failing Dennis   255
Ostreona, Queen of Mollusca   257
The semantics of reality   259
Quandary   261

Part Five

Grackle's reckoning 265

Animus 269

Tom Emmens, RIP 271

On learning 272

Chance 275

Brain farts 276

Prostrate in advancing twilight 286

On being a barbarian 287

Fugue in *Bu* major 290

Approaching homeostasis: the "perfect" world 292

Carnage of war 295

Doing good by doing well 296

A funny story 299

Spontaneous anarchy: a walk in the park 301

Lacking Polish polish 306

Support our troops: a deconstruction 307

In the dark 311

Aesthetic parameters 312

Sadhana 314

No help from heaven 315

It (all) is 317

Intoxication 318

Forgiveness 320

Let us give thanks 323

Part One

Grackle's cadenza

The mass of men lead lives of quiet desperation...
Henry David Thoreau, *Walden*

Lurching erratically through the portal of his eighth decade Grackle Pisswing was starting to think he was a melancholic. He was pretty sure of it, actually. When he was being candid with himself, he could see it had been coming for quite a while. One might even say he'd earned his stripes. Bummed with the current course of the whole civilization experiment, it didn't take formal training in psychic maladies to see it. He started a list to document the bases of his malaise, the winter, spring, summer, and fall of his discontent, to try and make sense of the situation. This is what he came up with:

From the general to the specific, the whole interdependent complex of life on earth isn't making it too well.

Humanity is looking increasingly like a parasite on the rest of the biosphere. In terms of virtually every other life form, we humans are a plague in every conceivable way.

In terms of intra-species conduct, along with a weakening of collective identity, there seemed to be a coarsening of human interaction, particularly in America, where people are apt to draw the in-group/out-group circle much closer than what was commonplace within recent memory. It may have been that in years past, most people assumed strangers were unknown in-group members until they demonstrated out-group tendencies, e.g., dishonesty, selfishness, ethnocentrism. Nowadays it seems people are inclined to consider strangers as de facto *out*-group—with more caution, as perhaps not having one's best interests at heart. This stiffening of the terms of human connections coincided with a groundswell of peripherally conscious awareness that society was about to enter a period of profound change, which corresponded to the increasing isolation, alienation, atomization, and apathy felt so pervasively in modern life. Subconsciously or consciously, people were anxious about future prospects. It seemed abundantly clear to Grackle that people had every justification to be seriously alarmed.

In his advancing years, Pissing appeared to draw a harder edge, too often exhibiting a blunt, insensitive, opinionated response to his interlocutors, reinforcing his isolation, no doubt. He had been moderately successful by society's standards. Married for 35 years, he was father to three adult children, all flourishing in the opposite corner of the country, with families of their own. He taught English for ten years in Japan, a Confucian culture where teachers are well paid and well respected. Semi-retired, he tutors English at a community college, as much to stay involved with young adults as for the money. He follows an unremarkable routine and is generally low profile in public. He had maintained a rich blend of social contacts, including six or so close vacation-binge buds, but over the last six or eight years three of them died and another two, likewise calcified and irascible, had soured, adding to his sense of alienation.

There it is, anyway: Disgruntled by his personal lot, doubly so by our collective circumstances, sinking into the fetid morass of geriatric angst. In a humane society, say, Scandinavia, he'd be evaluated and if warranted, an appropriate therapy would be available. Here in the Land of the free, home of the brave, since mental illness is not tangible or quantifiable like physical injuries or diseases, short of overt menacing behavior, people are quite literally left to their own devices. Got chronic funk? Suck it up!

Grackle was not presumed to constitute a physical threat to society, just himself. Potentially. Hard for society to generate a lot of concern for one aging malcontent Social Security recipient. The country of his origin, his Motherland, the political entity that he had come to routinely question the moral orientation of, sent him $600 a month: Biting the hand that feeds. How's that for irony?

Pisswing's fundamental beef with 21st century society was why otherwise-intelligent fellow humans, not couldn't, but wouldn't see the unsustainable impact humans were having on the rest of life on earth. Through sheer increase in population—tripled in his lifetime—but also by the increase of per capita consumption of essential resources, and subsequent increased production of effluents, human impact was venturing into uncharted territory. Never before would humans bear witness to such widespread species die off—including ourselves, presumably—we are at the precipice of. This recognition and acceptance of a significant population drop off during the imminent Great Unraveling changes one's outlook. With rare exceptions, nearly everything gets reevaluated through that lens. Social changes up to the tasks of reducing the carbon footprint, to say nothing of mitigating the habitat destruction humans wreak on the biosphere, imply vague but uncomfortable austerity at minimum, some ill-defined change in the wind. Thus, it's not difficult to see that willful ignorance is entirely here-and-now self-serving.

In Grackle's point of view, this basket of assumptions he'd succumbed to was an omnipresent curse, a misery that was downright Cassandra-esque, when approximately nobody else accepted its premises. Mainstream news to date, if it considered the issue at all, was mixed as to what courses of action would yield the best results—a further excuse to conduct more research and postpone any significant action. *Somebody else is on it.* And the longer nations postpone fossil fuel rationing, for one, the more certain and dire the unraveling. That specific disconnect to Grackle was particularly troubling.

The conquest of the earth... is not a pretty thing when you look into it too much.

Joseph Conrad, *Heart of Darkness*

One thing he monitored in terms of his psychic well-being was how his reaction fell along a continuum between annoyance, anger and frustration, and despair, hopelessness and despondency. As long as Grackle's ennui found a significant outlet in railing against this or that agent/agency or policy permitting, and perhaps encouraging, wholesale lurch into the abyss, his mental state was active and engaged in imagining logical and plausible responses to the current power holders. It stirred his passions. If you were not an automaton and you were convinced current human conduct vis-à-vis increasing fossil fuel extraction and consumption was suicidal, genocidal, species-cidal, and biocidal, then a certain amount of foreboding would be logically, if regrettably, a part of your outlook.

If you please, just don't permit that anger to slide into the black pit of hopelessness and futility; not so hard to do since, given all apparent data, the collective human predicament could very well be "futile," in terms of sustaining a social structure consistent with most of the norms we currently take for granted.

That statement is over-long and includes hedges, all of which tend to obscure the harsh realities we face. In essence, Grackle reluctantly concluded that social structures organized as nation-state entities with free-market capitalism as the primary economic model were fucked, and there was little we were going to do about it.

> *...every sort of consciousness, in fact, is a disease.*
> *Can a man of perception respect himself at all?*
>
> Fyodor Dostoevsky, *Notes from the Underground*

A profound anomie-minimization mechanism, a sirens' song, especially given his incipient physiological decrepitude, was to shrug off the whole 10,000 year collective human experiment as a fatally flawed event, one doomed to failure owing to the propensity of *Homo sapiens* towards outsized egocentrism, and its even more destructive counterpart, ethnocentrism. This stance required acceptance that the whole experience had been "destined" to collapse, and the sooner we acknowledged and acquiesced to that fact, the quicker resignation became the default position, and the better off our collective mental state would be. Something akin to the "Eat, drink and be merry for tomorrow we die" mindset. Or as a pop song would have it, *I've got a mind to give up living and go shopping instead...*

Grackle felt very little affinity with fatalism. Determinism, as he understood it, had essentially zero appeal for him. Even if this decline-and-collapse scenario ultimately demonstrates itself to be true, there is no way to show it a priori, and Grackle was having a hard time surrendering to it. He was a mensch; he resisted this resignation with every unreconstructed synapse of his skewed consciousness, even though it was surely a large component of his anxiety, his out-of-placeness, his painful disaffiliation with his culture/nation-state, and ultimately the entire "civilization." Still, the argument in support of kicking back and passively watching the de-evolution of civilization—especially so for one so late in life—was seductive. The argument implied, among other things, that old people of his ilk should surrender power, influence, and authority to the next generation, presumably in their ascendancy these years. However, the irascible Grackle was not yet ready to cede the national or global narrative to any other group—be that generational or otherwise—without his participation. There was an element of stubbornness, in this context, that comprised more pride than anything useful or practical.

...what you thought you came for
Is only a shell, a husk of meaning
From which the purpose breaks
*   only when it is fulfilled*
If at all. Either you had no purpose
Or the purpose is beyond the end you figured
And is altered in fulfillment.

T. S. Eliot, *Four Quartets*

To his horror, he was beginning to conjure a sympathetic identity with Kafka's reviled insect. Was this mental "metamorphosis" rendering him into an odious creature in the eyes of the general public? In the story, Gregor Samsa felt alienated from a rapidly changing, less-intuitively cohesive or meaningful society. His society, a century ago, was seen to be more menacing. If one's outsider status signaled revulsion on the part of society at large, it's not hard to imagine the psychic transformation he underwent, from a stranger in a strange land, to a sub-human, then finally a non-human. In Prague, in the period between the World Wars, the run-of-the-mill cockroach could very well have been the most hated creature, and arguably worse than rats, since rats are at least fellow mammals. But not a situation to aspire to, at any rate. In the story, Gregor's sister felt sorry for the giant roach her brother had become, and brought him food.

Grackle's sister Maggie sent annual Christmas cards, appropriately seasonal bromides, as the primary family connection through the decades.

A friend with some experience of the psychometrics used by state law enforcement and the judicial/penal systems had sent him web access to the standard psychic evaluation tool of the trade, the Rabbit Psychopathy Check List, Revised. On a whim Grackle decided to plumb this device for evidence of his own mental skew. However, made quite explicit at the outset of the material was an unambiguous admonition: *Under no circumstances is the reader, as an untrained amateur, to self-administer this evaluative device!* Also, a warning that casual application could result in significant misdiagnoses, or words to that effect. Clearly what the Rabbit Institute accomplished with this announcement was exoneration from legal liability.

With a certain amount of trepidation but no corresponding hesitation Grackle eagerly read through the material, at first to get a sense of how the metric worked, and then launched a full-court search for glimpses of his own insipient degeneration. He accepted that his crude self-evaluation was not likely to yield much specificity, yet even so, trends/inclinations could contribute insight as to one's psychic state. Not surprisingly, he did discover manifestations of "abnormalities" from one of the metric's categories.

In a later iteration of the psychometric Rabbit and associates identified two factors; within each was a set of traits that had a high correlation with one or another variant of psychopathy. Under Factor Two, Grackle seemed to have aspects of antisocial personality disorder (ASPD), perhaps "social deviance"—depending on how it was defined—and a higher risk for suicide. To be fair, however, it should be noted that other aspects associated with this Factor Two psychopathy diagnosis did not seem to apply to him: neither "low socioeconomic status" nor being a "sensation seeker, or easily bored" fit his lifestyle in any specific way.

Grackle made no effort to conceal his long-standing disassociation from mainstream-dominant values of materialism: greed, possession, and avid consumption of goods and services. *It's full speed ahead for the resurrection of the economy, and our grandkids' generation will just have to sink or swim according to their own devices. Just don't stop us now!* As a result, our Mr. Pisswing, a latter-day Don Quixote, made it a point whenever possible to demonstrate by his demeanor that he was other than mainstream America, and made no overt show of competing for social status or recognition. In a strange way eccentricity provided him a modicum of confidence and dignity. It was a way to show a little creativity in the way one chose to stand out from the cultural "center." Moreover, he was aware of the risks associated with living on the outskirts of the herd: You become easier pickings for the predators.

His stance tended to make him seem misanthropic, which corresponded with a degree of antisocial behavior, or perhaps just indifference. This was not the result of a character flaw or a mutational lack of the essential genetic makeup of nation-state chauvinism. Rather, he cultivated this stance. It was a conscious effort. He was reconciled to appearing an utter fool, or perhaps a *Ronin*, a "warrior" without master or a socially acceptable guiding principle. According to Grackle, very little of the core of America (as touted by the dominant narrative: all media sources, church leaders, and politicians of every stripe, et al.) was worth showing much respect for, so why continue the charade?

A more fundamental question: Is it psychopathy to display frustration and opposition to national policy when the society in its current form and function is demonstrably a cancer, blind to the fact that its "success" posits unending growth, leading inevitably to its own destruction—along with a large portion of the rest of the biosphere?

If so, thought Pisswing, *you've got me dead to rights.*

Personal disavowals

Don't tell me can't, you don't know
you can't until you've tried.
And having tried before is no bye
from trying again, now. Tell me
won't if you must: What you will
not do I can accept.
But own it; don't let unable
mince/prance around
obscuring its authentic self:

                            Will

                                not

Letter to the President

Mr. Barack Obama
President of the United States
White House
Washington DC

Dear Sir:

Congratulations on your reelection! Since you worked so hard to be elected President (both times) it is safe to say you have higher aspirations than to captain a foundering ship of state. But there is an increasing possibility that you, or your successor, will preside over a disintegrating nation, despite some efforts to the contrary.

Our country seems to be in a deep malaise of various sources. To be sure, the major surface issue is the floundering economy and its impact on the livelihoods of so many people. But another, rarely-publicized source is a growing recognition that the volatile and increasingly severe weather events we've experienced recently can be traced to our lifestyle choices—and this is only the beginning. People everywhere are spontaneously making small-step adjustments/improvements in their habits of material possession and consumption (i.e., reduce, reuse, recycle), and every step is important and valuable. But, to put it bluntly, none of them is going to matter in the long run, if we don't address the single greatest threat to our environment and our own well-being: the limits we are encountering in biospheric carrying capacity colliding with our burgeoning human population—from 2.3 billion to 7.3 billion, *tripled* in my 71-year-old lifetime.

The double whammy of more and more people, together with ever-higher levels of consumption per capita—with the resultant larger carbon footprint—make life on our finite turf more precarious by the day. We humans will achieve balance/homeostasis in one of two ways: either by design, i.e., electing to restrict our own growth (in both senses), or said balance will be visited upon us by some latter-day iteration of the Four Horsemen. It is becoming painfully clear that, given our collective resistance to anything but superficial alteration of our familiar, comfortable lifestyles, we are rapidly headed for the second outcome.

If I may be so bold, sir, I believe it is your job as Chief Representative to listen to your constituents, not your corporate sponsors, but We the people. You are to winnow our hopes and fears in conformance with the most thorough, comprehensive, and plausible science available, and enact stewardship policies on behalf of your daughters' and my grandchildren's future. A note of caution, however: the most shrill and strident voices, those who sound the alarm at the proposal of any significant change, no matter how practical or needful, do not deserve to prevail in this contest to safeguard a semblance of our national identity. The herd does what all herds do; they reinforce the group's desire for the status quo, if not a return to the good ol' days—ignoring everything but the immediate "pasture," according to the construction of the dominant narrative. The longer we continue business as usual; the more we squander our moral and monetary treasury on an out-sized military, vesting far too much of our national identity in a macho-belligerent military stance, yielding indefensible and ruinous foreign wars; the longer we advance the plunder and waste of the Earth's basic resources of air, water, topsoil, forests and fisheries—well, sir, the closer and more abrupt the financial and social collapse.

Some bold ideas are called for along the lines of a 21st century Moon Launch, or Manhattan Project, except with a minimum of hi-tech whiz-bang. A 10-year plan, that's 2022, to reduce overall military spending by 50%, reduce the personal and especially corporate carbon footprint by 50%, strip subsidies from BigAgra and Mega-Corp Beef/ Pork/Chicken, and give them to sustainable, individual/community agriculture and livestock raising. Subsidize renewable-energy development in place of fossil fuels, and underwrite all forms of mass transit.

Up-to-date versions of the New Deal's WPA and CCC could serve as models for a public service commitment of two years to a revamped AmeriCorps of all able-bodied residents between the ages of 17 and 24. This young-adult resource pool, in order to fulfill a civic commitment for "full emancipation," would learn to be socially responsible, as well as productive. Such Citizen Trainees might engage in small-scale public works construction, and all manner of infrastructure repair and maintenance; entry-level staff of hospitals, libraries, parks, school aids; care of elderly/homeless; disaster response/relief; sustainable farm apprenticeship, to suggest just a few. This movement, or something like it, could go a long way in restoring pride to our beleaguered country, and building confidence in a range of practical skills, perhaps principally cultivating the nearly lost art of getting along with people very different from oneself.

But ultimately, sir, all such measures are palliatives, mere extensions and postponements of the ultimate outcome for us Americans—and perhaps for us *Homo sapiens*, as well. What we need is a global saturation campaign to promote postponement of parenthood. Domestically, we need strong incentives to adopt, and a graduated taxation for each biological child. Bill McKibben, and many reputable scientists, suggest that climate change will cause serious-but-survivable disruptions at 350 ppm of CO_2 in our atmosphere. We already have +/- 390 ppm—and climbing. With climate change beginning to ratchet up and peak oil showing signs of summiting, rather than peaking these years, we need to use progressively less carbon-based fuel, but instead, as you know, we are using more. More of us, plus a higher rate of consumption per capita, equals more effluents/heavier impact on the biosphere.

As with the CO_2 model, it is quite possible, that in order to achieve a renewable-energy-based, homeostatic civilization without wholesale biospheric collapse, there should be fewer humans, at a more modest carbon presence, than we have today. Instead, to repeat, every day there are more of us.

There's a phrase that keeps coming back to me, said to have been uttered by Ishi, the last surviving member of a distinct community of indigenous people in central California, ca 1914— just a century ago. When asked to consider the many applications of technology the white man was able to turn to his advantage, how dominant his elaborate gadgets allowed him to be, Ishi's response was, *Smart but not wise*. Is this, or something like it, to be our epitaph? If we are merely waiting for one or more of the Four Horsemen to show up and make those "adjustments" for/to us, perhaps we aren't even as smart as we thought we were, to say nothing of wise.

The times call for a courageous statesman, sir; more of the same only dooms us to a bleaker future. Make it a collective call to arms. Pull out the stops. From the ground up, let's launch the rejuvenation of a sustainable America.

Urgently,

Tuna Cole

(posted November 15, 2012)

Long hair and the art of disabusing first impressions: on choosing the fringe

A little eccentric? Yeah, I know. I work at it. Arguably my hair is my most conspicuous affectation. Until we talk past formulaic greetings. Then one is apt to discover other—ahem!—eccentricities…. But back to the hirsute issue: Why grow it long? The flippant response, in view of all the tonsorially challenged, is because I can. And exactly speaking, I don't grow it long; it grows itself, unwilled by me—I just don't cut it very often, or very much. Gotta watch it, though. Eccentric is just a short step away from subversive—capable of devious, aberrant behavior. A threat to society.

A facile observation is, long hair on adult males in late 20th/early 21st century America is not mainstream dress code. Well, it's not even mainstream or core fashion for females of my age. But, by that same mainstream element, given the personal freedoms we are begrudgingly accorded in this multiethnic society, long hair on men is variously tolerated, endured, even accepted here and there, but rarely celebrated, with the exception of the arts.

So why would someone choose to appear eccentric (literally, out from the center), a conscious anomaly, someone willing to stick it out there from the first encounter? A limelight freak? Someone who's "on stage" most of his/her public life? Without trying to divine percentages, I guess an equally relevant question is why does a large proportion of society try to appear as anonymous and inconspicuous as they can muster, i.e., as close to their perception of the center of their cultural identity as achievable, to lose themselves in the group, while another segment does its utmost to demonstrate the distance they feel from the core of their culture. What's the dynamic here?

These two poles seem to be competing and "zero sum" in nature: Centrifugal vs. centripetal forces. What accounts for these divergent tendencies? Different "world views" at bare minimum. It would be foolish to ignore the importance of one's cultural identity and one's stance to it.

In my case, I choose to stand out/away from many of the values of my country (leaving the distinction between country and culture moot for the moment), as expressed by the mainstream narrative, the popular media. I so stand because there are too many instances on too many issues with which I absolutely do not indentify/agree. Though it sounds trite, I stand with the common person against the consolidation of power and wealth among the plutocrats, against the profiteers of war, education, health care, and the environment.

Long hair on an older male does not necessarily equate to such a stance, or any other, for that matter. Still, if a careful survey were conducted, I would expect to find a statistical correlation between so-called progressive values and long hair on a man. My intent is to wave disaffiliation like a self-cultivated banner at the herd animals surrounding me. To thumb one's nose at the automatons. If you've got it, Bubba, flaunt it!

I see more tattoos and pierced flesh these days than ever before, to say nothing of some pretty amazing hairstyles, and it's no longer just the young and the hormonally unbalanced. One is apt to see permanently-adorned individuals well into their 30s and 40s, even into theirs 60s, albeit in diminishing percentages. Clearly, there are many ways to use one's body as kinetic art. In a healthy society where diversity is respected, one would expect to find gender and generational, as well as individual, differences in self-expression. When it comes down to it, we all march to a different drummer, dance to a different beat.

Identities: *who'dja say you were, again?*

After all these years, I've pretty much decided I'm not who I say I am. I'm not a Tony. I've got a vague sense of what it means to be a Tony, having been delegated the role all these decades, and I've got an even better notion of what Tony isn't— that's me. I pretend to be a Tony and I manage it well enough. But I've just never really settled into the name—or it's never settled into me, one way or the other. It could've been worse: I've never been fond of the name George—since long before the halfwit former occupant of the White House was appointed. But I'd rather be lost in phonologically improbable, polysyllabic Pashtu family nomenclature than accept that one as mine.

A mote of family history here, how I came to be called Tony in the first place: I'm actually Carl III. My birth certificate reads Carl Anthony Cole, to distinguish me from my father, Carl Haggin Cole, and my grandfather, Carl Henry Cole. My father was called Carl all his life (well, my mother called him Hag) and I never heard how it was, two people answering to the same name, growing up in his family. The issue was avoided altogether for me since everybody's called me Tony from day one—long before I had the sense, to say nothing of ability, to head it off. Well, I'm here to tell you that just because people call you Somesuch doesn't make it you.

So here is an exciting opportunity for you to participate in a fun-filled contest. It's called, Help this fool find a name! Yes, you too can make an important contribution to your community (aesthetics? Mental health?) at virtually no cost to you (though financial contributions are accepted; ha!). You can help mold a psyche! Simply dash off a list of the most fitting names that come to mind when thinking of yours truly.

Warning: though I understand the temptation, all overt ad hominem, bestial, and anatomically impossible references will be elided. Let's strive for images that are optimistic and hopeful—or at least neutral—personal experience of the subject in question notwithstanding. Names that spring to mind "unencumbered by the thought process" (as the NPR Car Talk guys would say) are generally seen to be more valuable than cognitively tortured renderings. So don't waste another minute! This offer expires all too soon! Every reasonable submission considered; none forsaken, no matter how meager! Anonymous submissions permitted! You've got nothing to lose!

A final note to those of you who are casting about for the fine print in which it is explained how such a replacement name is to be winnowed from all the suggestions. Not to mention the nature of the reward. Alas, you search in vain. No panel of experts will convene; no august sage will be consulted. This will not be a committee process. In short: my dilemma, my solution. Should you be the lucky one to have your suggestion chosen, your reward will be the quiet satisfaction of hearing my new appellation in play...

The following constitutes a partial list of cunning variations of my name—a mind at loose ends!—my email correspondents have had to endure (Hey, Shakespeare went nutso with his name too, right?): Ant Oni, Antonym, Ynot, Tunis, Tunnel, Torny, Tonus, Tinny, Atonal, Toony, Tawny, Metonymy (as bullshit unwieldy as this appears, believe it or not, it's a real word; look it up!) Tunasty, Toeknee, Nyto, Tuna, Tonio, Anthem, Tyno, Tonacious, Betone, Tunes, Otny, Turney, Tunificent, Ant Enna and Onthani.

(June 2005)

Alpha/not alpha

Not (just) anyone
Either Tuna   this only
here-and-now me
or everyone   the everywhere
nameless and always
faceless everyone

Paterfamilias buffoonius: a projection

What kind of creature is my father, what manner of beast? Does not believe in a (Christian) God, and his loyalty to his own country, the USA, is highly suspect by his own admission (see other epistles). If he weren't my flesh-and-blood father, it's doubtful I'd choose to have anything to do with him. Ain't life funny? To be related by blood to someone so profoundly different. Just another lost soul, of which, regrettably, the world harbors too many.

I

So what the hell does he subscribe to/believe in? Calls himself an ethical relativist; what in God's name is that? How can some behavior or act be considered morally praiseworthy in one instance and be condemned as evil in another? Either it's good, once and for all, or it's evil. No hedges, no qualifiers.

Thinks he's flexible, open to other interpretations of reality. Sounds like a synonym for wishy-washy or fickle; a person with no principles, an opportunist, seizing whatever advantage he can. Says he's a secular humanist; an excuse for "anything goes." Secular means unattached to religious organizations, and humanism would seem to promote the notion that whatever people (humanity) want must be ok.

A crackpot hippie, is what he is. Got no respect for much of anything. A case of arrested development; never out-grew the 1960s. Thinks if everyone would just kick back and smoke a little ganja, the world would be a better place. Imagine if everyone tried to live like that! How irresponsible can you get? Some people just never grow up!…

II

Were it only so simple. I truly wish it were that linear, logical, objectifiable, and comprehensible (the all-encompassing non-human pronoun it: life, the world, reality, being, purpose, or?). Like everybody else, I yearn for a human community where strife is unknown; where harmony prevails because the people know and respect basic social tenets. Like everybody else, I'd love to buy into a system or process that could deliver this harmony. Lord knows, there are enough of these propositions out there: Some of them august and venerable, somber and steeped in ritual; some "new age" eclectic and all touchy-feely. And I'm as culpable as the next person in going to great lengths to avoid using my brain. (I'm convinced we humans devote more attention, court more distraction, actually exert more effort, avoiding/resisting mental work on a particular task than the task itself requires.) Unlike a lot of other folks, however, I can't seem to suspend skepticism enough to let these hucksters and charlatans get a shot; sure enough, sooner or later they all seem to put their foot in it.

To the extent we can and do get along is a marvelous thing. We should celebrate the instances of any kind of accord, be that one to one, family to family, community to its neighbors, nation to nation. Because, while we desperately need a sense of tolerance and compatibility with our fellow humans, thus far we have an absolutely execrable record of achieving it. Sooner or later the venal and corrupt, the elitist and self-promoting, the ego/ethnocentric begin to manipulate the more benign and trusting. I am not resigned but we seem to be conspicuously incapable of sustaining trust, compassion, and parity with our co-occupants; everybody's got a variant of, "If only everyone else would follow My (or Our) Way, the world would live in peace." That doctrine has failed spectacularly. So far, that canon has generated millennia of unremitting suffering.

If we can't agree on, say, the attributes of a deity, wouldn't it make sense to back up and try to locate similar or parallel views/needs that might promote a sense of harmony? You know, focus on the notions of "reality" we share in common rather on that which separates us. For millennia the primary source of spiritual and, more importantly, ethical clarification and guidance has been the religious institutions. From that historical fact, must we assume humankind is incapable of creating a constitution/bill of rights for all humans—and by extension, all life, outside the realm of this or that religion? Considering the overall importance of a framework of basic rights and responsibilities for all humans, I can't see why more socio-economic capital isn't invested in bringing that about.

(Fall 2003)

Inferences about the dominant narrative

It serves no good to continue to consider the *dominant narrative* (DN) as somesort of vague abstraction, perhaps nothing more than a construct of liberal paranoia. We benefit by identifying relatively discrete elements/aspects of the message; as a result, we begin to discern the not-just-plausible-but-likely intent behind the message. Ultimately, this exercise should provide us with insights in constructing a meaningful, relevant oppositional narrative. Here, then, is a tentative account of, and response to, some of those elements.

The dominant narrative represents the case for <u>centralized control</u>. Despite occasional superficial rhetoric on behalf of states' rights/local control, administrations show varying degrees of intentional consolidation of power. So basic is this aspect of consolidating more power in the hands of fewer people that it has been a bedrock canon of the political narrative for millennia. Certainly throughout Democrat as well as Republican administrations and their predecessors since our founding days (e.g., *The Federalist Papers*). The *Dubya* administration's power grab was among the most blatant and craven in American history with the suspension of *habeas corpus*, along with many other examples.

In order that centralized control be sustained, an obedient, uncritical, apathetic citizenry is required. Apparently, this is not difficult to accomplish after decades of hyper-consumption, the entertainment industry being arguably the most successful form of "consumption." Current Americans are the most entertained people in history. Seduced by any number of bedazzling distractions, we've become spectators, as opposed to participants, in our own destiny. The corruption of our elected representatives, when the story is told in any detail, becomes just another show to watch, an acting out—*details on the 10 o'clock news.*

What might the polity be like if the DN were successfully challenged, and permitted a *de*centralized, or local power structure? Authority could reside locally/ regionally with power and influence radiating outward. Distant (geographic, political, economic, cultural) regions and communities would have less influence on our area than neighboring regions and communities. And reciprocally, our influence would have less effect the more distant it became… Yet these somewhat utopian fantasies seem quite far from the type of society we are expected to pledge fealty to.

One of the mechanisms utilized by the DN to promote an Us-vs.-Them conception is the notion of a permanent state of war. First, a brief historical overview: On the heels of the 2nd World War, we found ourselves embroiled in a war against Communism (in which Korea, Vietnam, and Afghanistan, among others, constituted "hot" flare-ups in a 40-plus-year "cold" war engagement). To counter/ neutralize the threat that Communism was presumed to pose to our way of life, administrations and willing legislators saw to it that America's military expenditure and capability was essentially equal to the military expenditures and capabilities of the next 20 nations in the world *combined!* The age-old guard against one's enemies has been military buildup, and America's military preeminence has been accomplished at great cost. How long can the American taxpayer afford to underwrite the USA as policeman to the world, at the expense of our own schools, community health care, public transport/roads, and other public works? Stand by; this information should not be long in coming.

The 21st Century's equivalent of Communism is Terrorism. We've declared permanent War on Terrorism; it's perfect! There's no longer a specific nation-state willing to overtly harbor such *evil-doers*, whose ideology entails *hating freedom*, hence, no uniformed, identifiable enemies with nation-state allegiance (they don't fight fair!). Born of poverty and hopelessness, such people arise from many cultures/nationalities. Without offering specific geographic targets to attack, they are nonetheless sufficiently ambiguous, amorphous, diffuse, and ideologically driven as to serve as sources of great fear—thus, another important element in the DN: Be Afraid! Fear is enormously unifying. We unite behind strategies we hope will defeat or marginalize enemies capable of perpetrating attacks like 9/11/01. We fear a repetition.

Another issue of importance to the framers of the DN is how to treat wealth generation. It's clear that Wealth Accumulation, accruing to an increasingly smaller percentage of society, is more desirable to the DN than a more equitable distribution of wealth. On the one hand, we have the characterization of America's native entrepreneurial spirit tapped out, the creative talent blunted by the heavy taxation of a bloated and wasteful government (*We the people*) bent on hobbling America's ingenuity. In which, implicit acceptance of systemic inequality must also be the case.

In support of such a notion, witness the "weasel logic": One merely acknowledges that poverty and suffering have always been with us; that the issue is very complicated; that international agencies have been grappling with such issues for decades (if not generations!) with only limited success—it then becomes presumptuous for one person to think s/he might have a positive impact, a personal effect. Thus, willfully denying the patently obvious condition that people are *not* born or grow up with equal opportunities; that we fund programs to help level the playing field; that a society's social services are the ways in which we care for our less-fortunate members; that we tax the rich because that's where most of the money is. (Where did you think it would come from, *corporations*? Ha!)

If we hope to have a more egalitarian, democratic society, we must think of ways to narrow the gap between the inordinately wealthy (over $1 million per person in gross assets?) and the barely-surviving/not-making-it masses. At minimum, if we can't collectively begin to address this issue, our democratic republic is a sham.

Environmental Degradation, while not the explicit goal of any political agenda, nevertheless is the consequence of free market capitalism, *the* DN, constrained by nothing but the profit margin. Unfortunate though it may be, it seems nothing dare stand in the way of furthering/extending our economic prosperity. In the Pacific Northwest, under the guise of job protection and industry support, taxpayers regularly subsidize the plundering of our national forests, inasmuch as the costs of cutting, hauling, and milling these trees, then replanting, too often exceeds the market value of the trees, themselves. We'd much rather pollute and dam up our rivers, and throw vast ecosystems into crisis, thinking these are nothing more than the unintended results of human development —while our once majestic salmon runs languish toward extinction. Other examples of "externalized costs" abound.

The <u>Capitulation of the Fourth Estate</u> may well have been the final straw. True, the First Amendment to the Constitution guarantees us the *right* to free speech, the freedom to assemble where we choose, and the right to a free press. It by no means mandates it. Corporate sponsors, advertiser/clients, and owners of the print and broadcast media, have taken measures to minimize instances that the public see/hear/read unfettered and unflattering accounts of America's presence in the world. This corruption of journalists—our professional watchdogs, witnesses to the machinations of government, and primary sources of information—has been accomplished via the carrot *and* the stick: A) Reward the obedient and obsequious with privileged access to high-ranking officials and policy makers, in exchange for accepting the administration's scripted text uncritically. And conversely, B) punish the muckrakers: Exclusion, harangue/persecution, and/or arrest might await journalists critical of the regime—tending to make journalists docile sycophants of the power structure. Our principled investigative journalists in short order are rendered uncritical and compliant, abandoning their primary duty to the American public—to report as clearly and straightforwardly as they can the policies and events that affect the public.

So where does that leave us? If the logical extensions of the dominant narrative, via its identifiable elements, trend toward (in its most abject scenario) the collapse of the civilization known as *Pax Americana*, then we'd better be about constructing a point-for-point alternative narrative—the *Alter*Narrative.

Not just being, but me

When I can stop being
me, that is to say,
in those brief interstices
where/when I can step outside
myself and snatch a glimpse
of me as others might,
I seem to regard myself
too seriously, a little too
vested in my own take
on things to recognize space
for alternative takes. It must come off
as pushy and arrogant. At these
fleeting moments I feel
regret, remorse and embarrassment.
But soon enough I get back to being,
and not reflecting on being, being
an ongoing self-reinterpretation.
To one and all, sorry. Sorry.

(Summer 2005)

The effective, affective element in discourse

Isn't it interesting how emotionally vested some people can get in some issues? We all go there from time to time. Some more often than others, and some of those more intensely. Off the top of my head, it looks as though a few factors give rise to such fervor. The first is the perception that one's treasured conviction is being assailed or imperiled, and hence, appeals to all one holds dear to muster in defense. The second is the fear of being recognized as "wrong" by others, especially one's peers. A possible third factor might entail the phenomenon of the "recent convert" of the passionately expressive champion, having newly arrived from a long-entrenched oppositional position. A fourth, curiously occurring to me after the others: the obvious success and effectiveness of this aspect of communication. No one mistakes the overall intent of the affectively-exercised individual; the forcefulness compels attention. In the face of such fervor, is an appeal to reason a waste of time? Counter-productive?

Apart from that, it seems to me there is an inverse proportion between the emotional investment and the actual amount of research, study, and reading/seeking out others' points of view on the subject. One could conjure the rationalization that one's opinions are more "authentic" when they coalesce in the murky stew of the individual psyche, untainted by the conflicting and distracting static of the outside narrative. And it would follow that those who diligently search out other conceptualizations for confirmation or—heaven forbid!—lucid refutation, are corrupting and polluting their thought processes.

As if one could have proprietary claim to an idea, which is patently absurd, right? That which is yours, what you own, is your interpretation of this or that idea; your articulation is uniquely yours. Not the idea, floating freely in the Nousphere, a part of a channel that has existed since humans first began to think abstractly. Ideas take on meaning and utility as people give voice to their representation.

Still, the strongest, most persuasive aspect of face-to-face communication is the affective element: Semantic choices that exaggerate, convey a strong bias; use of the voice, delivery pacing, prosody, facial cues, and body language to give the unmistakable impression of where the presenter stands on the issue. If the presentation is performed well, a predictable number of people will identify with the message because they admire, respect, were charmed, or amused by the messenger's pluck and style: the Sarah Palin Effect. Or the audience succumbs to the message of fear; people are apt to forfeit power to megalomaniacs on the basis that they make a forceful case for consolidation of power in order to effectively safeguard the Fatherland: the Dick Cheney Effect.

It would seem that affective elements trump logic and reason every time. Not only do we hear an emotional message in the tone and presentation, the interlocutor largely-unconsciously "reads" the signs on a limbic level. Semiotics refers to non-verbal communication going on around the syntactic/semantic content. Sustained abstract thought, via the cerebrum, occurs at some cost, and many would say, the results are of dubious insight or utility. Pretty much the rest of the brain is devoted to aiding the basic functions: "Do I eat it, run away from it, or do I fuck it?" Not particularly hungry, fearful, or horny? Then, "Let's go start a fight, kick some ass!" The Amygdale and Medulla oblongata, parts of the brain that we share with the reptiles, are what drive the hormones.

And you propose to stand against this magnificent, affective, hormonal organism with mere *words*?

Intelligent design? an apostasy

Right off, I'll concede that from macrocosm to microcosm, there does appear to be a level of organization to our environment. Particularly in the realm of life on earth can we discern intricate orders of balance, interdependence, and system integrity. Thanks to Isaac Newton, circa 1670 (to say nothing of Euclid, Archimedes, Galileo, and many others), we've come to understand many of the basic operating principles of nature. Events occur in patterns ordered with a degree of predictability—far from random. So the problem doesn't stem from the notion of design, per se. My strong objection arises from conjoining the notion of cosmic "design" with "intelligence."

Let's see if I can paraphrase the argument: Life is so intricately, interdependently designed that it could not have occurred by chance. Design implies a designer in the way that a watch implies a watchmaker. Therefore, there must have been a designer, someone (or some*thing*; English is poor at conveying this concept) must have designed the whole works, at least at the outset, and caused it to be set in motion—*QED,* a quick rendering of one of five arguments for the existence of God, as articulated by Thomas Aquinas in the 13th C., *the* designated hitter for the Christians for centuries.

Deep breath. Count to ten.

If you come at this *not* from the position of wanting to support a particular belief system but from wanting to understand/ explain natural phenomena in simplest, most comprehensive terms—*de*scriptive, rather than *pre*scriptive— then "created by God" is just obfuscation. It's additional baggage without yielding benefit. If the answer to why things (e.g., *women,* or pick your own anomaly) work as they do is, "I don't know"—the worst-case scenario: abysmal ignorance—then what is gained by having the same question *non*answered: "It's God's will; it's His (*sic*) creation"? This here earth was *Made by God*; end of inquiry. But who or what designed the Designer, created the Creator?

You're back to, "I don't know." Only this way, there is no incentive toward discovery: "God did it. Surely you are not presuming to question the will of God, are you?" In fact, you'd have to say there are pretty impressive *dis*incentives: Eternal damnation and/or burning at the stake (to hasten the journey). So my argument is, thus far, that a Designer is not a requisite for a design explanation, assuming we can agree on the parameters for design.

Warning, Christians! Proceed with caution! Here comes the E word!

The first thing about evolution, as articulated by Darwin and subsequent naturalists, biologists, et al., is that it is not at all a random process and thus, not the result of *chance*. In every case, to the limits of ability to respond to stimuli, organisms biologically "choose" to avoid the harmful and be receptive to the beneficial. Inevitably, changes to habitat occur; thus, another survival mechanism is adaptability. Those who don't adapt, perish—natural selection. And so on.

It's difficult to wrap your head around the notion of 3 to 4 *billion* years. That's at least 3,000 *million* years; folks who are working with a time frame for the whole universe of only six *thousand* years can't hardly do it. Even folks who buy into concepts of geologic time, I think, can only dimly imagine how fantastically long a time that is for life, however improbable, to begin, replicate, diverge, die out, begin again, replicate, adapt, replicate, mutate, replicate, reconfigure, and replicate, failing by huge margins before flourishing once. But we can see from many disciplines, e.g., paleontology, geology, archeology, biology, etc., an explanation for design, as perceived in life on earth, that does not rely on an externality that cannot be determined by empirical inquiry—an explanation that has a great deal of supporting data, from many different disciplines, to corroborate it.

But let's suspend rationality for a moment, play the "devil's advocate," and assume a Designer created it all, likewise suspending questions of His/Her/Its antecedent (or did this Designer/Creator produce Him/Her/Itself out of sheer *nothingness*? The mind reels!). In our culture, of course, this Designer is God the Father—Lucky for us! We were designed in His image (us guys, anyway). Regrettably, He's had to put many obstacles in our way to challenge our faith. We are to persevere in our faith and resist temptation because our reward of an eternity in Heaven awaits.

No doubt, our Designer/Creator loved all of His creation, and I can certainly see how many of us humans deserve a trial or three to help establish our suitability for eternity with God. However, here is the rub: The God-given mosquitoes which carry the malaria virus don't discriminate among the worthy-for-suffering adults and the wholly innocent children, kids as young as one or two, far too young to conceive of reverence for, let

51

alone defiance of, some mystical Being in an abstraction called Heaven, far too young to have a nascent faith tested by earthly suffering. Or consider HIV/AIDS, which has been argued (by shamefully mean-spirited, sociopathically ignorant people) to have been brought down upon licentious fornicators as punishment for their sins. However, is it an indication of the *intelligence* of the Designer that this virus be transmitted to the unborn child through the uterine wall?

Whole cultures ignorant of our Judeo-Christian religion have been brought low from any number of afflictions (cholera, tuberculosis, measles, typhoid, influenza, small pox, typhus, and syphilis, to mention the big hitters of the last 500 years), introduced by European Conquistadors, missionaries, traders, and colonizers—in the name of God. Recent calamities brought down upon us directly, the pure and wicked alike, by the All-seeing, All-knowing One include the Christmas, 2004, tsunami in SE Asia, estimated 300,000 dead; October 2005 earthquake in Pakistan, perhaps 75,000 fatalities; and Hurricane Katrina. Is there an orthodoxy, is there a morality that could justify the suffering of even one child?

What the Hell *good* is a God with all power, presence, and knowledge, who chooses not to intercede in cases of profound suffering? Who, in fact, *created* the suffering? I do not accept, in fact, have contempt for, an omniscient/omnipotent/ omnipresent Being that is AWOL, voyeuristically detached, watching the disasters we humans regularly visit upon each other, to say nothing of the rest of the biosphere. I take my cue from Bertrand Russell, Thomas Paine, Mark Twain and many others: I need a healthy dose of logic and rationality before I will suffer religious dogma. God-the-Father, as promoted by the Bible, is an inadequate explanation for life on earth and an unworthy moral guide. Intelligence without a sense of compassion, at least for the children, and those most vulnerable and innocent, is unworthy of reverence.

(Fall 2005)

We know very little

We know very little
We don't know very much
Many of us know that we don't
know Some of us don't
know that we don't know
From this latter group many
insist on demonstrating they don't
know Finally some of us can't
resist calling out those who feel
compelled to flaunt their ignorance
in exaggerated self-importance

Faith: meanings, applications and consequences
(for Andy and Lyle)

Faith is a widely misappropriated word these days, it seems to me. One might suppose it was bound to a particular application and thereby discredited in any other use. To be sure, the dictionaries indicate the association of faith with religion, inasmuch as it constitutes belief, sometimes with strong conviction, in a notion for which there is no empirical evidence. I have no objection to this definition, as far as it goes. It is only when there is an assumption that somehow faith is *exclusively* allied with religion that I take vigorous exception.

We often hear of "faith-based organizations," and so-and-so being "a person of faith," which in the current vernacular invariably implies religious association. The counterparts, "faithless" and "faithlessness," are even more objectionable since they suggest someone or group as having no moral compass, lacking a sense of right and wrong as applied to how we should conduct ourselves, and thereby unworthy of trust, belief, confidence. There is an element of ethnocentrism (*us vs. them*) inferred that one who does not believe in the same theological/ethical orientation as you do must have inferior guiding principles. Or suffer an absence of principles altogether.

I see no reason why such secular entities as a community's schools, its library system, a justice system which includes citizen jurists, its public transportation network, even its parks—aspects of our grand experiment in self-governance—can't be considered as faith based, albeit the faith involved relates to other parameters than belief in a supernatural power. I consider myself to be a man of faith, though I utterly renounce systematized, ritualized, hierarchical spirituality (religion). My faith relates to a loyalty, trust, hope, and constancy in ideas of social justice, and a belief in the possibility of the human family living in cooperation and in balance with the rest of the biosphere, despite scant evidence that said conditions are occurring.

This constitutes a pragmatic, secular ethic: Without this faith and hope for a better-balanced, more inclusive, cooperative future, I fear that I would be participating in this social experiment in a way that exclusively benefited me and my close circle of family and friends. Without somesort of conscience rooted in social justice (recognizing a need of wide latitude for interpretation), what would stop me from exploiting the vulnerabilities of my fellow humans, lying and cheating to improve my own wealth and status at their expense? Presumably, I could even "rationalize" such abominable behavior in the projection that my co-inhabitants would be plotting the same strategies against me.

I think the time has come for us hyper-social primates, we "great" apes, to formally adopt simple language to acknowledge and codify our responsibility to the biosphere. We will always have a significant impact on species and habitats just as they have on us; it's a symbiotic relationship. From micro to macro, other life forms die in order that we live, *naturally*. The danger is that our collective impact is now so omni-directional and colossal in scale that whole realms of species, micro-, macro- and meta-habitats are poised to collapse. We are courting wholesale species extinction.

Society's laws only discourage or prevent sociopathic behavior to a minor extent. The legal and penal systems give shrill testimony that, in spite of religious proscriptions against sinful behavior and societies' continual enforcement of laws, far too many people still believe 1) that they are unique and deserve to benefit at the pain and suffering of fellow humans; 2) they will evade capture/succeed at their crimes/sins; or 3), a version where many people find themselves without jobs, unable to find a replacement job, and soon unable to pay for food, shelter. In this third instance, in the face of deep hunger/deprivation a law against theft of others' property becomes a useless and easily dismissed abstraction. They quickly become desperate (*Wouldn't you?*), especially when children are concerned. As the saying goes, Desperate people do desperate things. One could argue that the "leaders" of society (in America, politicians, and the corporate moguls who control the institutions of social capital: the media, churches, financial institutions) got too greedy and failed to consider the bottom three-quarters of society. Alas, faith in religious doctrine of any stripe has thus far fetched up woefully inadequate to the task of righting these social injustices.

Is human nature really primarily selfish and self-serving, or do we have the capacity to live in tolerance, moderation and cooperation? Are we able to design through education and public policy a paradigm shift in our social organizations to achieve higher levels of social harmony, *and* a meaningful stewardship of nature? This would constitute a shift away from our age-old *intra*-species preoccupation to one of *inter*-species. There is a duality to this struggle. One self desires/celebrates the interconnectedness of self with many other lives, and intuits the

57

connection to all life, past, present and future. The counterpoint is the self who, acting out of isolation, desires power and prestige by whatever means s/he can get away with. Primarily, the natural resources, but fellow humans also, are means to an end for this latter self: the gratification of Number One.

For our future survival in a form remotely similar to what we take for granted today we'd better get started reducing our fossil fuel consumption, our carbon footprint. This is energy transition, certainly, and very probably energy descent. The sooner we accept this idea, the sooner we can make some progress on mitigation. It's essential we approach a stable, moderating impact on the earth and its interdependent life forms. It's difficult to imagine a more critical adjustment we face, and to prolong the discussion only makes the drop off steeper, more severe in consequence.

Not to put too fine a point to it, does it make sense to place one's faith in a supernatural power, either 1) taking care of/resolving humanity's "successes," which come at the expense of pillaging/ plundering the rest of life on earth, or 2) pointing the way in unambiguous terms? Given the data so far, faith in this *deus-ex-machina* outcome doesn't hold up to scrutiny. Wouldn't it make more sense to invest some hope, faith, trust, confidence in the peer-reviewed data on, say, climate change; scope, duration, and expanding consequences (feedback loops), and, based on this faith, begin to act accordingly? This might be characterized as faith focused on the present and near future term versus faith in the hereafter.

Our narrow, selfish nature and our more expansive, relational nature continue to play out with no end in sight. At a time when God/the Gods have given no overt indication that

He/She/ It/They care about how we humans fare in this dilemma, the focus of one's faith takes on critical importance.

Mir Ghat

By the time of my early evening arrival there was really only one fire vigorously burning, with three or four other smoldering remnants. A man came back and forth from the river with a bucket, dousing the coals of the all-but-dead fires, exploding billows of very fine, gray ash. When sufficiently cooled, the charred pieces of unburnt wood and bone were swept into baskets to be carried on the heads of two lowlier helpers to a pile at some point down the bank of the river, Mother Ganges.

The one blaze had been recently ignited, and I moved around to an advantageous perch from which to watch the event. In addition to the professional fire tender, there was a group of onlookers engaged in the management of this particular pyre. I took them for the deceased's family and friends for although they did not directly participate in the maintenance, they continuously heckled the fire tender as to how to better manage the blaze. Nestled in the bier of wood, the cloth wrapping the corpse had not yet burned through when I got there, but soon the singed-black globe of the skull was visible among the uncaught branches.

Out on the Ganges riverboats maneuvered throngs of tourists, all eagerly and morbidly snapping photographs of the spectacle. The only other living souls in the vicinity were an occasional cow wandering in complete freedom among the smoldering remains in search of some straw, or leaves, or a banana peel—anything with a little vegetative roughage and some wayward carbohydrates—and a few scrawny mongrel dogs, as is a common sight on any street in Varanasi.

It didn't take long for the fire to reach its apex, the smaller faggots reaching their kindling point first, then combining to ignite the larger ones until the pile was a crackling inferno, and the human form, wrapped in consecrated linen, once partly visible in the loosely piled rick of logs, was soon totally obscured by the towering flames. But, what was that poking out of the blaze—a foot? No, surely not. But yes, I could make out the digits. And the tender, in haste to have done with the job, rearranging partly burned logs, and with spirited jabs of his poker, so as to insure a faster combustion, tried to stave in the chest cavity and skull... One wonders where these people could possibly get enough wood to satisfy the need of the nearly constant ritualistic cremation along these river banks.

Enough! What manner of lurid temptation draws you to this place, and then compels you to stay and watch? You berate the tourists for wanting to witness, titillated, albeit from a safe and convenient distance, that which you seem willing to wallow in. Ah, but as I was leaving, to my dawning horror one of the feral dogs in the vicinity raced past me pursued by three others. I did not see where they came from, but that lead dog clenched in its jaws a segmented bone very much like a human knee...

(Varanasi, India, Fall 1966)

Two questions

Standing not at all
humbly before
the gilded, smiling Buddha
hearing the monks' sonorous recitation
of well-worn sutras pondering
what would man be
without his gods to serve?

Then striding out
from the quiescent shadows
of that much hallowed place
wading into the volatile tempest
the cacophony of the proximal/
temporal manswarm I wonder
where to go next?

(Bangkok, 1966)

Dark clots in the atrium:
a sorta gothic tale of (near) woe

It was a dark night at a secluded campground just below Lolo Pass on the Idaho side. It had rained the previous evening coming from eastern Washington, so the little lady and I moteled it in Coeur d'Alene. The next morning, driving out of the drizzle southeast into Montana, we must've dropped some elevation because it got a lot drier, not from the storm we'd finally outrun, but from the sparse vegetation—like eastern Washington before you get to Spokane. More-or-less skirting that ridge of Rockies to the west, we sailed through Missoula unimpressed with yet another big, post-war city spread to the winds/seven off ramps on the fornicating freeway, *maybe* self-sustaining post-Collapse at one/tenth the current population.

At this point neither of us had a specific destination in mind for the night, but prepared to camp if possible. We gave the map a quick consultation and headed south to the cutoff to Lolo Pass, the self-same passage Sacagawea guided Lewis and Clark through the Rockies, and saved their sorry asses. At the crest we got out to stretch our legs at the visitor's center; I've forgotten the altitude but in mid-July there was still snow in sheltered places. So it was, with shadows growing longer, evening approaching, we chanced upon this primitive, nearly unoccupied campground right next to the Clearwater River, just out of the vast Bitterroot Wilderness area.

Camp set up and dinner preparation went uneventfully; it's surprising how simple and complete a meal can be, how comfortable the camp, if some thought and preparation are employed. We polished off the wine and attended to post-meal clean up and still had time to take a walk along the river where we skipped some rocks and harvested some native blueberries. I'm reasonably attentive to the condition of the natural environment I put myself in; what manner of flora and fauna am I about to share this area with? Based on the "sign", there was pretty good evidence of deer and possibly elk browsing leaf and ripening berries here and there in the surrounding brush, but no recent bear scats, for which I was somewhat assuaged, since these mountains, unlike our western Oregon mountains, provide habitat and have resident populations of Griz (*Ursus horibilis*). As I say, only partially mollified, as I recalled the well-worn adage, *Absence of proof is not proof of absence.*

In our neck of the woods the only bear you'll encounter is a Black Bear (*Ursus americanus*). And unless it's a sow with a cub or two, you can run off a startled Black Bear through sheer crazed bluster. I know; I've done as much. But a Griz, especially one who's gotten used to the scent of food associated with humans, is fearless and can very easily kill one or two hapless campers in the night. If Br'er Bear thinks 1) the humans are food, or 2) they are obstacles to the food clearly in the vicinity, that might be all she wrote. The olfactory sense is generally more reliable than sight or hearing to a bear; they've been known to smell carrion well over a mile away. The nose knows.

I remember the evening was pretty warm; jackets were deemed advisable primarily as further protection from the flying bloodsuckers. (Isn't it interesting that only the females suck the blood of warm-blooded, and apparently quite a few cold-blooded, critters? Rendering an otherwise thoroughly pleasant experience an endurance of misery, or pursuit of escape?) As the light faded we put foodstuffs and cooking gear in the car, and performed the evening ablutions. Soon the fire with its flickering light was dying out and the mosquitoes were becoming emboldened—our signal to beat a retreat to our bug-proof tent, where sleep overtook us in short order.

Sure enough, a few, short hours later the nerves from my bladder started sending alarm messages to my brain—a phenomenon regrettably familiar to most aging men—too soon the ravaged dam was threatening to spill its contents. Nothing would do but to crawl out of my comfortable bedroll, slip on shoes, and step a few paces away from the tent to a nearby tree where the floodgate could be opened and the warm stream could sluice. Still a warm night with the merest hint of a breeze down the valley. I remember standing there an extra few seconds enjoying the peaceful ambience of the forest. Then, it was back to the tent where I nosed in and spun around to sit on my sleeping bag facing the opening, shoes still outside. I was removing my shoes when I noticed that my right shoe was quite wet, and so was my foot, for that matter.

My first thought was, in my evening reverie gazing off into the night, I must've micturated on my right shoe without knowing it. About the time my brain was rejecting that hypothesis on plausibility grounds, I started noticing a vaguely familiar smell that I couldn't quite put my olfactory finger on; a little cloying, not attractive but not offensive in the short term. Meanwhile my right ankle was still very warm-sticky-wet. Then it hit me: Blood. My *own* blood. I was hemorrhaging from a break in a skin-thick blood vessel in my right ankle. Again. In fact, this might have been the 4th or 5th occasion, going back to our *Meiji jidai no ie,* our old, traditional style cottage, in Kugenuma, Japan, pre '95. I had scraped it ever so slightly (by slipping on the shoe?) and standing up suddenly had sent a surge of blood to my feet; on previous events I was able to shoot a stream of blood nearly two feet horizontally.

The bummer for the wife was she had to wake up and help me staunch the flow, and attend to clean up. She hated it—could you blame her?—but rose to the need of the occasion. While I reclined to take some pressure off vessels carrying blood to my feet, she rounded up paper towels and extra water to do mop up. It seemed like a lot, but it probably wasn't more than a pint. The blood was still fresh so it came up pretty easily from most surfaces. Not so much with sponge-like material, like the inner surface of a sleeping bag; that would take professional laundering at a later time. She closed up the blood-soaked shoe and sock in the back of the car, along with the bloody paper towels, came back to the tent and, soon, went back to sleep.

I, on the other hand, lay on my side facing the zippered tent flap a mere six inches away in the gloom, and ruminated over my deteriorating physical condition. The smell of fresh blood in my nostrils, I became increasingly attentive to forest noises. Even on a still night, the forest is alive with sounds. See me there, twitching to the rustle of some brush over there, a twig snapping in another quarter. My aural vigilance was accompanied by a spontaneous series of spectacular scenes in my imagination, invariably concluding with one or both of us devoured by a ravenous and therefore surly bear. In one scenario, I was able to distract the bear by beating on its snout with a flashlight long enough for Betty to slip out of the tent and dash for the car. All in all, it was surely one of my more memorable nights.

Hours later, with hoary dawn in full onset, I finally drifted off for a precious hour of slumber. Breakfast and break-camp went uneventfully except to note the impressive, sticky, dull-maroon puddles of my blood, one where I'd intentionally donated another, far-less viscous fluid, and another one just outside the tent entrance—I had been completely oblivious until sitting down in the tent. *Had there been* a bear in the vicinity, it would be hard to imagine a more conspicuous invitation to a fresh meal.

In less than three months from that occasion, I would experience a scary phase of heart flutter, followed by the imposition of a curious chemical regimen including rat poison, culminating in having my heart stopped. *And...* started again!, thank you very much, the intent being to correct my atrial flutter. The rat poison, under the trade names of Warfarin and Coumadin, thins the blood to the point where it will dissolve a clot or prevent one from forming, due to the flutter never letting the atrial chamber to fully engorge, or empty. Once there was assurance no clot lurked, waiting to rush out to an ever shrinking channel—like as not, in the brain—where it would quickly jam the channel shut, then the procedure of shocking my heart into arrest, and almost immediately (after the team members wandered back from their coffee break) back to a normal sinus rhythm could take place. The year after that, after a phase of painful, heartburn-like symptoms, and finally ruling out food or indigestion as a source of chest pains, I am now the proud owner of a heart stent, a steel wire cylinder designed to keep at least that stretch of vessel free from near-term clotting. All, exciting bouts with the aging process.

But I sometimes think back to that halcyon eve of spontaneous blood-letting while camped in the Great Outdoors, and wonder if it would've been a kindness to future campers to have posted a warning of the un-clean-up-able blood puddles at that site. Immediately calling into question the wording of the text, of course. Accepting that the message contain some explanatory language, a couple of variants spring to mind:

1) *Be advised! A pint of fresh blood was poured on the ground in this campsite (Freedom of religion; consenting adults; arcane, venerable practices; phases of the moon, that sort of thing).*

2) *Warning! Up to a pint of blood was taken from an adult--not unlike our forefathers experienced to draw off their toxic humors—and deposited on the ground. What was good enough for George Washington is good enough for me!*

All I'm saying is there had to have been some curious nocturnal critters haunting that campsite for the next several nights.

Logos

In the beginning was the Word, and the Word was with God, and the Word was God... Gospel of John 1:1

You know, in my heart of hearts, I *love* words; especially when they're *my* words! Not neologisms of my own invention—though I could provide a few—but conventional words I've strung together into unique expressions. So in a sense, they are my babies very much like the living, crying creatures we birth—*of* me but not mine to possess.

I've got scads of words corked up inside because, in truth, during most of my life, I lacked the confidence that my words, crudely aligned, would have any truth/beauty/value. They were constrained from soaring, as they were wont to do, by the usual set of inhibitions: not wishing to fail, as we all feel in some fashion or another (the ignominy!). Furthermore, I've been effective at distracting the urge/pursuit for Logos.

A good part of the New Testament was written in Greek; logos in Greek means *word* from which we have, in English, *logic, dialogue* and *psychology*. And in its own way, that's logical since logic is dependent on words, via language, giving rise to communication of meaning and intent. An agreement of general terms and standards as to what things mean allows us to understand one another fairly accurately. Thanks to language we humans have been able to organize *our understanding* of the objective world; the more we've understood, the more we've "organized" the world around us to suit our ends.

Conversely, a lack of agreement as to the meaning of our "reality" is the antithesis of logic, i.e. chaos, if not anarchy in its most brutal form. Civilization throughout history has depended upon language and so, arguably, self-aware, social humankind "began" with the "word."

We differentiate sanity from insanity according to the degree one deviates from accepted standards of order, normalcy and meaning. Think what you want but if your *behavior* extends a trifle too far beyond those norms, then you are by definition irrational; perceived as a potential threat to the community because you are fostering chaos, or anarchy.

Logic is essential for the first of two basic functions of language: *to inform*. We mean the same when we direct or instruct; it's the imparting of information. Passive as well as active voice is also requisite. To inform implies the involvement of someone being informed; to instruct presupposes being instructed. The notion is a co-construction.

But it's the other, subtler purpose for communication that defines our humanity: our willingness and need to share, to grow closer to others through exchange of perceptions, ideas, feelings; our subjective as opposed to our "objective" nature. This, then, is to me the source of our true wealth, the myriad expressions of our joy, wonder, love, and humor. Even our pain, humiliation, rage and fear are authentic aspects of the human condition and contribute an important part of our identity.

My favorite word-picture painter is e. e. cummings:

worms are the words but joy's the voice
down shall go which and up come who...

So it occurs to me this love of language, the finely turned phrase, the well-constructed sentence, satisfies one of two basic conditions for becoming a person of letters: *Do I have something to say?* The answer is, at least for now, a cautious *yes*. The other equally important condition is, alas, not for me to judge: *Can I say it well (*i.e., *meaningfully, artfully)*? It's probably safe to compare writing to many another human enterprise: You learn to cook (well) by cooking; becoming a gardener requires the act of gardening, of running your hands through the earth, by putting thought to action. One becomes a writer by writing.

(Portland 1996)

Sunday in the park

Poised on a bench amid low foliage and small trees, two wrinkled and aged, black-shrouded widows are seated across the path from me. Among us, we occupy the only two benches in this modest park. An ancient tower commemorating Lycurgus—an Athenian leader, 390 BCE—rises behind me, and off to my left, an unassuming marble plaque states that Lord Byron lived bordering this park, 1810~11. The sound of children playing (Greeks and Turks?) fills the otherwise-quiet Sunday afternoon with sharp, clear outbursts.

Through slightly swaying branches above the toothless specters, I see a cat walk indolently over to a broken and roughly tiled roof. And high over my right shoulder soar formless cumuli above the contrasting sharp edge of the east corner of the wall of the Acropolis. The Parthenon is invisible from this vantage point; naught but the blue-and-white-hatched flag is visible of the summit. While I muse on these sacred heights, a third withered, beaked and shrouded *Yiayia* hobbles into our realm, regards me coldly, and seeks a place with the others, exchanging brief mutterings of recognition and greeting with her cronies.

I recall that the *Erynes* (Furies) numbered three, as did the *Eumenides*, promoted by Aeschylus as the *Kindly Ones*, renderers of justice for an evolving society. Furthermore, these women were said to be given residence somewhere below the Acropolis. A shrill cackle emitted by one at an observation by the others gives me small pause that my three observers from across the walkway could be the Kindly Ones from 2500 years ago.

72

Our franchise on this local turf is at last shattered when a couple of young lovers appear, hoping for a modicum of privacy, but settling for a piece of the bench next to me. After a polite few seconds for social adjustment, the interlopers can stand it no longer and commence lip-to-lip, hand-to-body contact, hormonally charged and desperate enough to be oblivious to the scrutiny, if not outright opprobrium, of their audience. It is an amazing event to behold. Quite literally their lust/love for each other (*Hey, who am I to say that isn't love too?*) eclipses every other affective experience going on in that setting.

Ora pou gamani oi yiphtoi.

(Monasteraki, Athens, Autumn 1965)

I get asked

I get asked by inquisitive people
What are you doing here?
My inclination is to answer
I don't feel I have to justify my existence
at this time. I'm living here, that's all.
Just living. Which is a copout upfront
a deferred response. So I thought
to investigate What it is I do   here
and Why to just about everything
in the context of discovering Who
I am thinking doing and being are related
Ha! Easier said than done
even though I didn't say it
worth a shit. Still looking, in a word
still taking measurements   refining calculations
analyzing the data   regretfully decline
a definitive response for the moment
get back to you   What?
You think *I* know?

Part Two

The media according to Grackle

According to Grackle Pisswing (and thus an unreliable source), television was the number one homogenizing and narcosis-inducing agent in the US. This insidious device was arguably the single biggest purveyor and articulator of the American *zeitgeist*, and by far the biggest distraction from the number one responsibility the media have historically always been charged with, namely, to report relevant and important news and information to the public in approximate objectivity and fairness. TV has been in long standing the number-one shill for corporations and their products, certainly based on advertising dollars, and it had come to be a parody of itself. One supposes as long as there are viewers, there's a buck to be made, to paraphrase P.T. Barnum, but the means by which that coin is being turned—the ads! The ubiquitous advertisements! What a telling denouement of what Americans are willing to spend their time and money on—and the level American corporate merchandizing has stooped to court perceived needs.

Prime time TV, network news at 6 or 6:30 pm, for a half-hour, has devolved into a series of brief commentaries of the affairs of the day surrounded by five minute clusters of ads, one crammed up against the next every thirty seconds. Grackle found it bewildering and vaguely hypnotic. It seemed to target the middle-aged and older—presumably those most in need of pharmaceutical/ medical attention, *and* most able to pay the cost—or quite probably the last major demographic to watch network TV at this time. The most frequently heard phrase across all manner of pharmacological advertisements was, *Don't delay! Ask your doctor about... Flomastibono Chlorodiphenabinol! It's good for what ails you!* (Sotto voce, delivered very rapidly)

Don'ttakethisproductifyouhaveconcernsabout   liverandkidney function.   Notifyyouphysicianifyouexperienceprolongedcardio/   pulmonary interruption...hasbeenlinkedtolesions/ulcerations   ofthesmall   intestines incontinence   ...lossofhearing...   compromisedvisual/ olfactory   function, generalized neurasthenia...

Remember Nancy Reagan's injunction? Just say no to drugs! Ha! Based on prime-time television ads, the whole nation is awash in drugs. Lord knows Grackle was doing his share, chocking down a fistful of pills morning and night. Pills to lower blood pressure—two kinds. Pills to lower cholesterol. At least one pill to mitigate the damage to his metabolic/electrolytic balance caused by other drugs. Then, some vitamins and minerals and herbals, like saw palmetto, said to have beneficial effects to the prostate. And a product called red yeast rice. An existence rife with absurdity.

For the national television audience, you've got your "body shaping augmentation" for those who have let themselves go far too long for the odd diet to make much of a dent. These clinics must accumulate barrels full of human fat all of it sucked out of the jowls, bellies and asses of morbidly obese customers. What's the responsible thing to do with this "byproduct"? Hopefully not flush it down the drain. Maybe they moonlight as a soap factory... *Boutique soap made from "all natural" ingredients!*

In addition to liposuction of all that unsightly fat, right there on family-time TV, we've got three different drugs to encourage stud-like tumescence; I shit you not. We aren't actually treated to any visuals of the miracle happening, the rebirth, as it were, but pop these pills right here, and we are assured that when the moment is right—as for example, in the midst or repainting the dining room!—one telling glance, a wink and a perky *Buy me a drink, sailor, and I'll tell your fortune*— and you can get right to it there on the paint-dribbled dropcloth without any mood-trying coaxing necessary.

You got your *Machogel*, a salve… to be applied where, exactly? The ad guys on Madison Avenue must've knocked themselves out on this one. The background consists of an all guy work crew, noticeably advanced in age, but yet suitably virile, setting up with the help of heavy machinery, giant concrete-like numerals followed by a percentage symbol. Apparently the FDA had allowed the manufacturer to boost the amount of billygoat "essence" from a mere one to a fantastic 1.62%! So while a mature adult male extols the virtues and efficacy of this increase in potency, the bunch of men all past their prime are busy erecting these giant numbers using chains and hooks, and other manly gear. Let's face it; guys don't shy away from work that needs to get done! Just one of an array of potions designed to boost the thrust of one's rocket.

In another ad a fading movie star is having a conversation with her pals—the topic? *Irregularity!* Irregularity of *what*? you might well ask. The term on its face is vague enough to include one's menstrual cycle, sleep rhythm, or the periodicity of one's sex life, but no, it's code for the evacuation of one's bowels. Via gesture Ms. Celebrity is quite demonstrative of what she means by taking her sponsor's product and restoring her digestive track to regularity. Placing her hand near her chest, fingers and thumb all aligned and pointing straight down, she extends her arm downward to nearly its full length, at which time she swoops out from the body about crotch level like an F-16 coming out of a dive: *Release the floodgates and stand back! Here comes the brown tide!*

How many families—Mom and Dad, Dick and Jane—are sitting around the dining room table, having dinner while watching the evening news? (Too many, to be sure.) So here's a couple of examples to shatter the idyll. Surely none of these families deserve their daily dose of global catastrophes to be served up (*some more mashed potatoes, dear?*) with penile salve to facilitate on-the-spot sex for aging roués. Furthermore, it is hard to imagine these salt-of-the-earthlings need their meatloaf garnished with the hard sell (again!) of chemicals that promote outgoing tides, so to speak, to match incoming ones, medicines to keep the *in*crements in balance with the *ex*crement.

Timing of the presentation aside, who'd have thought such a huge proportion of society would have such chronic difficulty simply defecating? Thanks to the combination of an urban-centered/ more sedentary lifestyle, and a generally more refined food diet than our grandparents, this simple act has become an ordeal... *and* an opportunity to make a buck! The point is, it's your life, goddamn it! Just keep tucking away whatever the heart desires. Don't you let anybody tell you what you should and shouldn't eat. Does the diet tend to be a little heavy on the animal fats? We got a drug for that. A mote excessive in refined sugars and carbohydrates? Just take these pills, right here. Pretty soon, it's not at all unusual to need drugs to mitigate other drugs. Grackle Pisswing had experience of this phenomenon first hand.

An energetic, fully focused middle-aged man sidles up to the camera, asking *Do you suffer from du-rai ma-uth?* with a straight face, as if he expects us to take him seriously. No hint of satire apparent in the scenario, no punch line forthcoming.

Uh, as a matter of fact, yes, I do occasionally suffer from dry, sometimes called "cotton," mouth. What's it to you, stranger? Turns out Mr. Suave represents a liquid product that, if swigged assiduously, would sure 'nuff take care of that pesky ol' parched oral cavity. No word as to deleterious effects, in addition to the stated effect of alleviating a parched condition. More to the point, not a word as to cost. The fact that this product is pitched on prime time TV tells us, 1) that there is a market out there; ad time doesn't come cheap, and 2) people are so gullible that they'll pay discretionary money for an unnecessary product, when probably the simplest solution you are apt to have for this particular ailment is a mere few steps away. Usually that stuff out of the tap will do the trick. *Dry mouth? Try water!*

When I'm watching my TV
a man comes on and tells me
how white my shirts can be
but he can't be a man 'cause he doesn't smoke
the same cigarettes as me...
Rolling Stones, *Satisfaction*

Despite our recent preoccupation with personal electronic computing and communication devices, regular ol' movies in physical theaters were not bowing out at all quickly, owing in large part to America's unrelenting, insatiable appetite for distraction and self-delusion—in its basic form, *entertainment!* Carefully wrought characters in complicated scripts have tended

81

to give way to elaborate computer graphic fantasies. It was often hard to see the connection from the visual imagery now routinely possible in films to the mundane reality surrounding him. But that was the point; the less grounding in the familiar, the more fantastical, the better. Give us more and better escape! To paraphrase Pink Floyd, we've become comfortably numb.

Cleverly crafted stories with complicated, ambiguous roles don't rock our world anymore. We want our tales stripped of extraneous details, and given to us as a cartoon sequence. We happily surrender sophistication, depth, and context in the story for more mayhem, preferably fast paced and violent, especially among our more hormonally charged citizenry. If it's an urban setting, we're going to need at least one massive car chase, many vehicles destroyed—miraculously, with no innocent bystander or good-guy casualties! If it's rural and woodsy at all, we require some exotic weapons, preferably the really big-bore variety. Animated films were once the stronghold of Disney, pandering to children and the child-like with neutered and sanitized fantasies from Brothers Grimm and Mother Goose. In the last decade or so animation had become increasingly popular and profitable, appealing to the so-called adults by featuring death and destruction.

Another example of our ability to endlessly distract ourselves is the recent development of "cage fights." Since ancient times, civilized societies have promoted boxing and particularly wrestling. Neither of these "sports" could be said to be humane, yet they are Olympian sports. The explicit object seemed to be to hurt one's opponent to the point that he would capitulate, cede victory to the dominant athlete. Even as kids, Grackle and friends knew professional wrestling was staged. But there were rules, no targeting the groin, for one, and the combatants were pitted against each other more or less according to weight classes. Open cuts/bloodletting were grounds for suspension of the match. And no matter how sickened one might feel by such an event, hoary tradition all the way back to the ancient Greeks and the original Olympics was a persuasive legitimizing factor. Cage fights, however, took the violence and brutality to a new level. Both gladiators were secured in a steel cage; no time outs, no 15 rounds punctuated by breaks. Only utter defeat—or complete victory—signaled escape from the salivating, screaming spectators and the caged battle site. Blood? *Oh, yeah!* Broken bones, cut lips, smashed noses/jaws? *You bet!* The audience has paid good money for such a spectacle, the more, the better!

Thus, we see Grackle's willingness to exaggerate the narrative here and there to confirm his biases. Much of the preceding regarding cage fighting is factually inaccurate. A figment of his lurid imagination.

Profound self-aggrandizement not only yielded a higher incidence of psychopathy, but not coincidentally a diminished/ attenuated sense of community. No doubt we have the capacity to take into account the interests of self <u>and</u> the interests of the society as a whole. That said, however, the more we emphasize empowerment of I/me/mine the less legitimacy the entire social framework seems to warrant. Notions of the collective whole take it in the neck if all we are about are personal freedoms/rights. The irony is we are fundamentally going to make it *together*, or we're not—going to make it. *What an ironic, vicious, rotten state of affairs*, thought Grackle.

All the knowledge in the world
is not worth one child's tears...
There is suffering, yet there are none guilty.

Fyodor Dostoevsky, "Brothers Karamazov"

Another of Grackle's peeves was ignorance. How can that be, one might ask, since every mortal is significantly lacking in whole realms of knowledge, and thus it would always be. It was surely not possible to know enough not to be ignorant. No, the ignorance Grackle railed against was the lack of knowledge of simple, immediate, everyday power relationships—and the grotesque, misplaced pride that accompanied this brand of ignorance. This was gratuitous and wholly unbecoming of a responsible citizenry, but an increasing percentage of his fellow Americans flaunted the disparity. Typical Americans knew more about the current crop of celebrities and their recent scandals than basic knowledge of the Bill of Rights, or the Vietnam War just one generation prior, or the current machinations of the government. To Grackle, this represented a serious misappropriation of values, an unfathomable disordering of priorities. This stance, no matter how injurious to a self-governing society, was vainly manifested as a citizen's "right," even if the consequence meant the ultimate decay and collapse of America's pretense of government of, by, and for the people. One certainly had the right to ignore even mainstream, superficial analysis of the workings of our government, and it appears many people exercise that right. Ad absurdum. One supposes, a person has the right to bash himself in the head with a hammer, if he is dead set on doing it. Does anyone think that would be the correct, productive, or meaningful course of action to take, despite one's personal "empowerment" to do so?

As far as he was concerned, people were gulled into reflexively having "pride in America." He thought the notion was preposterous. One could, if one were sufficiently self-absorbed and vain, take pride in a personal accomplishment the community valued. Get a promotion at work? Achieve a 4.0 grade average? Earn another Scout merit badge? Well, bully for you! Yet, viewed in the cultural/national context we can say being American was contextually peripheral to it. Really, what does your citizenship, the geographic location of your nativity, have to do with your accomplishments? Essentially nothing, except to serve a different agenda.

We could say that our democratic, representative system of government, and our Bill of Rights, permit us opportunities not available in many other countries. Not all other countries, mind you, but the point is acknowledged. The thing is, nobody chose to be born, period. To say nothing of being born male/female/ Navajo/Creole/Latina/LGBT, or whaddya got? Grackle thought it was a trap to get suckered into notions of patriotism and pride in conformance with national identity, milked shamelessly by the jive-assed, jingoistic election-time politicians in heat. Furthermore, branches of the nation's armed forces were not above crude macho chauvinism. The way Grackle saw it, if you *earned* the achievement through your effort and determination, then a degree of pride, a modicum of crowing was understandable and acceptable. That in no way extended to attributes of who you are: gender, ethnicity, sexual orientation, nationality, and the like. You were born with-and-into these characteristics; they were aspects of your being here and now, but not a matter of your choosing. Of course various specific policies, laws, rulings were eminently worthy of challenge—some even of praise!—however, identity with one's motherland was outside the realm of pride or shame.

No doubt that *Pull together for the good of the country* mentality helps to unify the citizenry, a useful identity pretty much only when the motherland is under attack. Otherwise, why pull together instead of pull apart? Or keep it flexible, *Lucy Goose*. Why one big US of A and not a lot of little ones? Alternatively, why not a "one-world federation"—a US of T: United States of Terra—without sacrifice of local sovereignty? Is bigger ever better? If so, when, and under what circumstances? Because we know without a scintilla of doubt that bigger, faster, and ever more is absolutely *not* better considering human impact on the biosphere…

Grackle was convinced America had become too big and unwieldy. Too big to fail meant the entity ought never to have become that big in the first place. By the time America's representatives were elected, having successfully run the gauntlet of lobbyists with outstretched hands bearing wads of cash, they were clearly no longer beholden or responsive to the needs of the people. Time to banish private money in politics, and reinterpret the "states' rights" clauses in the Constitution. Better yet, start anew with a focus on a federation of cooperative, virtually autonomous sovereign entities. His advice was, Cut through the *Proud to be American!* crap, and get down to more fundamental issues about who we are and who we need to be in relation to the rest of the biosphere… Not because we feel a personal bond with each and every imperiled species (utterly impossible), but because our own continued existence on the planet in any meaningful sense has always depended on our relationship to the interdependent web of life.

Even through his profound disappointment with the unrestrained impact of his species on the biosphere, Grackle still felt *attachment* for his species, these fellow creatures so full of vanity and pride, his kin. Certain of humanity's accomplishments, when considered from within a strictly human perspective, were indeed worthy of deep respect. Among our many accomplishments, Grackle thought, music of all genres represented an apotheosis of the magic humans were occasionally able to conjure, though to be sure, he was enriched by and proud of a large array of artistic expressions.

Also, he was proud and grateful for his forefathers—regardless of ethnic origin—who were able to employ scientific discoveries to enhance human life. But, it now seemed apparent, much of that power came too easily and we became drunk on it, particularly petroleum. Now our addiction to, and profligacy with, fossil fuels is propelling us toward the Abyss. Climate change is upon us, only to get worse, possibly for many centuries, even if we were to stop producing greenhouse gasses today. And we ain't stoppin' *nothing*, baby.

The Anthropocene Era—named for us in recognition of the profound effect we have over the rest of the biosphere—looks to fulfill the prognosis of being the shortest epoch in geologic history, a mere blip in the Holocene.

Ketchup

(Impatience)

I stood on a rail, balancing,
while it and its parallel counterpart
streaked into western infinity
of still-glimmering dusk.
Suddenly FosterKleizer's incandescence
burst artificially onto a giant façade
bright red artificial bottle
of Hunt's ketchup emblazoned
with a bright red artificial tomato on the label.
Pictured next to the bottle, by comparison
of excellence, was a bright red artificial tomato.
I was amused thinking of the parallels:
inside in the lounge on their coffee break
my fellow (artificial?) workers
were praising the purchase of a brand new
white (but not chaste) metaphorical Mustang
whose proud owner, Epicurus,
had just mortgaged his hypothetical soul
for 36 months. In seven
I'll be in Greece!

(ca 1965)

2005, the Golden Anniversary of rock and roll

A milestone has recently passed: 2005 was the 50th anniversary of the emergence of rock'n'roll as a distinct genre of music. Yes, boys and girls, it was 1955, the year I started high school, that, in terms of popular music, "Tin Pan Alley" gave way to Carl Perkins (*Blue Suede Shoes*), Johnny Cash (*Folsom Prison Blues, I Walk the Line*), Elvis Presley (*Heartbreak Hotel*, après le deluge), Chuck Berry (*Maybelline*, followed in quick succession by *Brown-eyed Handsome Man, Roll Over Beethoven, You Can't Catch Me, Johnny B. Goode*, and about 15 other classics), Fats Domino (*Ain't It a Shame, Poor Me, Don't Blame it on Me*, and many more), Bo Diddley (*Hey Bo Diddley, Who Do you Love*) and the pillager of all musical icons up to that point, the embodiment of sheer bestial exuberance; I'm talking raw, unconstrained, adrenal lunacy, the Georgia Peach hisself, Little Richard (*Tutti Frutti*, chased rapidly by *Long Tall Sally, Slippin' and a Slidin', Lucille*, and some twenty more).

I

Where did these guys come from? It was as if, on a national scale, they suddenly appeared on the jukeboxes and on the popular radio stations. Popular music in very short order made a giant shift away from songs that tried to capture images of mainstream life and romance from the point of view of professional adult songwriters. In their place, the mid-1950s youth market was strong enough to support (in sales of, at first, 78 rpm acetate records, then 45 rpm vinyl singles, and LPs) singer/songwriters fresh on the scene, barely past teenage years themselves, who catered to their dismissive and defiant style.

True, Fats Domino had been around for some years; in fact, the New Orleans-style piano/saxophone upbeat jazz crossover held forth from Jelly Roll Morton, Professor Longhair, and Huey Smith as direct antecedents/contemporaries to Fats. But the rest of these cats just exploded on the scene without warning, caught us unawares, mouths agape, in shock. Like Pallas Athena bursting fully-formed from the forehead of Zeus:

A wop bop alubop a lop bam boom! Music was changed forever.

II

I bought a brand-new airmobile,
'twas custom-made; 'twas a Flight de Ville.
It had a powerful motor and some hide-away wings,
push in on the button, you can hear her sing:
You can't catch me. No, you can't catch me,
Cuz if you get too close, I'll be gone like a co-o-ol breeze!

New Jersey Turnpike in the wee, wee hours,
I was rolling slowly 'cause of drizzlin' showers.
Here come a flat-top, he come movin' up with me,
then goes wavin' goodbye like a little ol' souped-up jitney.
I put my foot in my tank and I began to roll,
moanin' sirens, t'was the State Patrol,

so I let out my wings and then I blew my horn,
Bye bye, New Jersey, I become airborne.
Now, you can't catch me…

Flyin' with my baby last Saturday night;
wasn't a gray cloud floatin' in sight.
Big full moon shinin' up above;
cuddle up, honey, be my love.

Sweetest li'l thing I've ever seen;
I'm gonna name you Maybelline.
Flyin' with the beam set on flight control,
radio tuned to rock and roll.
Two, three hours passin' by;
count those tunes up to 505.

Fuel consumption way too fast;
let's get on home before we run out of gas.
You know, you can't catch me.
No, baby, you can't catch me.
'Cuz if you get too close,
I'll be gone like a co-o-o-o-ol breeze…

Cars and chicks and lookin' cool; what else was there? Well, counting coup on the establishment, for one thing. Chipping away at the granite edifice of the powers that be, the adults, the entrenched status quo. Maintaining one's cool while taking a position in opposition to the dominant narrative. *They* stood for rules for the sake of regimentation; stultifying, soul-robbing behavioral expectations that were slowly, inexorably, turning us relatively free, open, budding *optimal people* into creatures like *Them.* The Horrors!

So fight it we did as, I suppose, every generation has against its predecessor. In our case, the fight was immeasurably aided by rock'n'roll. I learned from the music, particularly Little Richard, that the basic, elemental source of power came not from a rational performance, no artful narrative, but from the direct appeal to the senses. I mean, really, who could understand Little Richard? To this day, I couldn't tell you most of the lyrics of any of his hits. It ceased to matter immediately after I gave up trying to fathom the meaning and relaxed into the freight-train tempo.

Arguably, Mr. Penniman's biggest contribution to popular music was the introduction of the full-on shriek. Prior to this man, in 1955, no one had ever screamed to signal a pause in the lyrics, which were, as we've noted, far more a frame for his *voice* than an expression of content. The affective realm of rock was more personal and direct, bypassing the cognitive function altogether, and it seemed to demand an emotional response— usually one of sympathetic identity—or of utter repudiation. There was no middle ground: either you shut off the radio and closed your mind to that mother lode of emotive power, or you surrendered to the thundering avalanche, and hung on for dear life.

Then, again, try Bo Diddley:

> *I walk 47 miles of barbed wire;*
> *I got a cobra snake for a necktie.*
> *I got a brand new house by the roadside*
> *made out of rattlesnake hide.*
> *I got a brand new chimney up on top*
> *made outta human skulls.*
> *Come on, take a little walk with me, Arlene,*

an' tell me who do you love?
Who do you love, who do you love?...
Gotta tombstone head and a graveyard mind,
Just 22 and I don't mind dying,
Who do you love?...
I rode around town, use a rattlesnake whip,
Take it easy, Arlene, doncha gimme no lip,
Who do you love?...

What is this, verbal foreplay? This guy is trying to macho-intimidate foxy Ms. Arlene into balling him, more like it. The opposite of sweet-talkin' her, I'd say. Through various narratives, by various blues/rock artists this was a not-uncommon approach to seduction, the troglodyte approach. Seriously, perhaps they meant well, but weren't they starting off on wrong foots with variations of, *I'm going to make you* (her, him, depending on the agent/object) *mine*? How, exactly, were you thinking about "making" her yours? Sounds deviant; a high potential for abuse via the built-in inequality, the dominant/submissive relationship. One imagines the scenario of a parent making one's teenage daughter/son clean up his/her room before s/he could attend a desired function (i.e., sanctions imposed by the authority), but that somehow doesn't seem to capture what the song is about...

III

Well, it's a one for the money (a-dun dun),
two for the show (a-dun dun),
three to get ready, now go, cat, go,
but don't you step on my blue-suede shoes.

93

You can do anything but lay offa my blue-suede shoes.

Well you can knock me down, step in my face,
slander my name all over the place,
do anything that you wanna do but,
uh-uh honey, lay off of them shoes.
Cuz don't you step on my blue-suede shoes.
You can do anything but lay offa my blue-suede shoes…

I had a pair of pink suede shoes. I musta been 15 and I was Hot Shit! Except that I hadn't learned much about limits or balance. (What, *me*? Overstate something?) Besides the shoes, I also sported pink corduroy pants, a pink shirt with faux-gold cufflinks, with which I wore a black bow tie sporting pink pokadots. A black belt was the only other contrast, with the tie, to… *Pinkman*! I might've worn black socks but I think they were pink, too. Truly a sight to behold. Astonishing, in retrospect. It's only from the vantage point of 50 years that I can revisit that time without cringing in embarrassment.

I worked hard during Christmas vacation delivering complimentary calendars for the upcoming year, sponsored by the local mortuary. That is to say, I toted those calendars house to house, block by block, and negotiated being driven to new areas to canvass. So I'd earned the shoes. In short order, I'd acquired the rest of my ensemble and soon began appearing in public (school dances, primarily) thusly attired. Alas, it was not an entirely salubrious experience in that I was neurotically self-conscious on top of being four-eyed, pudgy, and pimply, on the cusp of puberty. And here I was, outrageously calling attention to yers-truly: Mr. Teenage Pink, Pimply Pimp. I suppose this episode could be said to be a harbinger of my emergent willingness to flaunt the status quo, to embrace eccentricity—literally, taking a position away from one's social and cultural center.

Despite my dazzling raiment, however, the comely damsels did not flock to my side, lips pursed, eyes almost closed, swooning, entranced. It was just another experiment in vanity, mercifully short-lived, but it contributed to the realization that I needed to work on who I was, the core me, and tone down the trappings. No doubt, I still need to attend to my identity but not to the desperate extent of my sixteenth year when glimpses and snatches of meaning and purpose, other than those that revolved around depraved, carnal lust, of course, were few and unsustaining.

You shake my nerves and you rattle my brains
Too much love drives a man insane.
You broke my will, but what a thrill
Goodness, gracious, great balls of fire!
I had good love and I thought it was fine;
you came along and moved me, honey
I changed my mind, this girl's fine
Goodness, gracious, great balls of fire.
Kiss me, baby. Ooooh, feels good!
Hold me baby; I want to love you like no other should
You're fine, so kind;
got to tell the world that you're mine, mine, mine, mine.
I chew my nails and I twiddle my thumbs.
I'm real nervous but it sure is fun
Come on, baby, you drive me crazy
Goodness, gracious, great balls of fire.

Like Jerry Lee, my insanity took the form of craven lust, except, alas, my experience was by way of a succubus, painfully unrequited save through the soothing ministrations of Rosy Palm and her five daughters…

IV

Even in those days, there were chinks in the American Dream. Being a less-than-perfect social structure, an experiment undertaken by less-than-perfect humans, it's fair to say there always have been. Ten years after the cessation of the most inclusive, widespread conflagration in the history of humankind (World War II), despite America being pretty much at the top of her game, fissures in the "Ozzie and Harriet" mainstream projection of the ideal family life were starting to be noted. Sometimes, one really couldn't buy the outright homilies and platitudes; sometimes it was impossible not to notice that the mantra, *Work hard and success awaits*, simply did not apply to certain racial and ethnic groups. Sometimes one size really doesn't fit all. It is worth noting that within a week of my matriculation at Sunnyslope High School, Phoenix, AZ, in Montgomery, AL, Rosa Parks refused to give up her seat to a white man on a public bus. As a triggering incident, her simple act led directly to the long-overdue civil rights amendment.

Employing humor and oblique irony to the reality he witnessed and endured, Chuck Berry was the most creative and successful rock satirist of the time. Perhaps of all time.

> *Working at the fillin' station; too many tasks:*
> *Wipe the windows, check the tires,*
> *check the oil, dollar gas!*

Ahh! Too much monkey business,
too much monkey business,
Too much monkey business for me to be involved in.
Blonde half-goodlookin', tryin' to get me hooked.
Wants me to marry, settle down,
buy a home, write a book,
Ahh! Too much monkey business,
too much monkey business...

And just sheer, cocky chutzpah about the power and the appeal of the music he was putting his stamp on:

I'm gonna write a little letter,
gonna mail it to my local DJ.
It's a rockin' little record I want my jockey to play.
Roll over Beethoven, I gotta hear it again today.
You know, my temperature's risin',
the jukebox blowin' a fuse,
my heart's beatin' rhythm
and my soul keeps a singin' the blues.
Roll over Beethoven, tell Tchaikovsky the news.
Well, if you feel it 'n' like it, go get your lover
Then, reel and rock it, roll it over,
an' move on up just a trifle further
And reel and rock with one another.
Roll over, Beethoven, they rockin' in two by twos...
You know she wiggle like a glow worm,
dance like a spinning top.
She got a crazy partner, you oughta see 'em reel and
rock.
Long as she got a dime, the music won't never stop.
Roll over Beethoven...

Roll over, Beethoven, indeed! As in, if Beethoven could hear this jive, he'd be flopping in his grave like a newly landed mackerel on a boat deck. More than any other musician, Chuck Berry set the tone for all rock guitar artists to follow. Without this 1955 birth, there could have been no mid-to-late-60s Second Wave. Without these First-Wave cats, there woulda been no Beatles, no Stones, no Zeppelin, no Who, no Clapton, no Jimi, no Janis.

Tell Tchaikovsky the news!…

Toward a secular ethic

Realizing that I am a mere mortal and not especially gifted, at that, no one should be surprised or disappointed that I don't have a Unified Field Theory of Ethics. Not just yet (Ha!)— but if it comes about at all, it will come about through tolerant people. Tolerance is practical, after all; it underlies the means of getting along, respecting each other's cultural orientations, patiently building commonalities. The benefits of cooperation should be obvious.

No "socially unifying" manifesto will come from petty power exercises among entrenched belief systems—prominently, organized religion; equally prominently, nation-state chauvinism. People are not likely to cooperate better on issues vital to us all through manipulated sentiments of kill-or-be-killed situations a la "defense of the fatherland;" patriotism being an over-wrought, spent mechanism for keeping the citizenry riled up, distracted, and polarized. There is no longer any *Them*. There is only Us.

For better or worse, all technological advances have been based on a rational approach of applying empirical events to human advantage. Such advances, along with the boom of the petroleum economy (peaking these years?) have thus far been able to "support" 7.5 billion humans, skipping for the moment a look at the ratio of the truly rich compared to the truly wretched. Then there's the case for humankind choking on our collective "success," but considering our impact on the biosphere, it is virtually unfathomable to think of any other basis than reason for mitigation, or solution. If applied reason (i.e., technology) got us to this predicament, we need to apply reason to a few more variables in minimizing and mitigating our impact on each other, as well as the rest of the biosphere.

Inasmuch as humanity's collective impact has been both unrelenting and ever expanding, various signal species and networks of species, on which we directly and indirectly depend, are pushed to the brink of collapse. We are exceeding/have exceeded the carrying capacities of myriad species; we're compromising whole ecosystems.

Thus, it behooves us to create a set of standards that respects not merely all of humanity, but ultimately, all of life. These standards should be of our own design, with no presumptions of divine inspiration, and we should all take responsibility for them, separate from, and having precedence over, any orthodox religious practice individuals may choose additionally. Allow me to offer some candidates for the 21st C. Decalogue. Or whatever it turns out to be.

I) Everyone is different at some level and, at another level, everyone is the same. One individual/group is not better or worse than another, only different. Act accordingly! Act as if you have something to learn from other customs, other ways of interpreting the universe.

II) An important human sameness lies in the fact that our lives, our continuing survival, depend on our designing an approach to homeostasis with the rest of the biosphere. This must begin soon! Failure to launch fundamental and, many will say, drastic changes will bring catastrophic results; if we procrastinate, postpone, commission more studies, dither much longer at current rates of rapine, it is a 100%-sure bet homeostasis/equilibrium will be reached independent of us through biospheric collapse. Or, in other words, mass extinction.

This is the world we find ourselves in: Our predecessors, generation after generation, applied technologies and fossil fuels to ever-greater human advantage with scant public dialogue as to possible consequences. Nobody knows how long human consumption at current rates can continue before a perhaps-innocuous (to us) species collapse triggers cataclysmic flora and fauna die off the likes of which has been unknown since the Permian Extinction 250 million years ago, when something like 90% of life died out. Without significant portions of our biotic support to rely on, this collapse would presumably include us humans collectively, but especially us Americans, in that we comprise but 5% of the world's population but have become accustomed to consuming over a quarter of the world's resources. Furthermore, for a very long time until very recently, we've had the dubious distinction of being the world's foremost polluter, by various measures. It will enhance our own survivability, to say nothing of many, many other species, if we take this seriously (as if our lives depended on it!) and begin to live more modestly.

Our level of indulgence is not an entitlement. It's a cautionary tale with increasingly obvious signs of what it will be like to live beyond the carrying capacity; the consequences are just beginning to come home to roost. J. H. Kunstler, of *The Long Emergency* (2005), believes we've already entered the decline of the petroleum economy. I think of it as the "thirty-year flip": the period of time it will take for most social structures to devolve to self-sufficiency, coinciding with a population collapse, a period of great suffering and death. Whether we humans make it, in any

101

meaningful sense, is going to depend on how quickly we can create and adjust to essentially self-sustaining communities, with human-wrought climate change wreaking havoc all around, sharing overlapping niches with many life forms not yet adapted to the environment they find themselves in. Brave New World, indeed!

Epilogue

Note, there has been no mention of the *Rapture* in this assessment/projection; there is simply no empirical basis to consider the Second Coming of Jesus Christ seriously. Those of you who would take exception to this last statement, counter me on the merits of the assertions offered, not by articles of faith— otherwise, you're not really talking to me; you are talking to others who share your beliefs. Let's create a text that is inclusive, not exclusive. We need to act together as if the Earth's resources are all we've got, and not act half-expecting divine intervention. *We* need to take responsibility, not rely on some pie-in-the-sky deity that belongs among humankind's assorted fables.

God in one

God in one and the one in all
but does it matter at all?
Cognition entails measurement;
measurement, a point of reference.
How to take stock of oneself
without counting, naming;
drawing contrasts, similarities.
Nobody believes there's nothing
to believe in

Allegiance: a hierarchy of identities

I no longer pledge allegiance to Old Glory. By my reasoning I don't owe primary, supreme allegiance to my native country. This may sound heretical (if not traitorous) to many. The knee-jerk response is to assume if one's allegiance is not to one's mother country, it must be to another nation-state—conspiring against one's homeland, as it were. In my case, however, I feel my first allegiance is not to my mother country or to any other nation-state, but to the biosphere, the vast and intricate network of life, including us and on which we quite literally depend.

An inter-connected web with all the habitat-interdependent microcosms within the Earth's macrocosm, the biosphere is as yet little understood. Most of the understanding accrued to date has been at the behest of wealth and privilege, which circumvents nation-state sovereignty. This emerging knowledge of "how the world works," for the most part, seems to have been applied to extracting resources as quickly and as profitably as possible. To the extent I am aware of these dynamics of production and consumption, I try to minimize my impact. A biospheric collapse graphically demonstrates catastrophe for all the spheres within it. To bear witness to inequity and fail to act is to be complicit.

My second allegiance, in subordinate position to the biosphere, is my responsibility and allegiance to our species, a component of the biosphere. Though the "success/prosperity" of

Homo sapiens may not be challenged by another/other species currently, I have a vested interest in the survival of humanity. (We humans may be short lived, however, if it turns out we lean too heavily on too many other species.) From this perspective, my allegiance and commitment to humanity comes before any nation-state, even my own, in the instances, actions, and events that would seem to privilege one national entity at the expense of other constructions of humanity.

Allegiance number three, subsumed within species and biosphere, is to my culture(s). The issue is complicated by the fact that, especially in urban areas, people choose memberships with various groups/tribes/cultures to reflect multiple interests, skills, and identities. Is membership conferred, are we born with it, or do we appropriate it? Clearly, it depends on the context.

The dominant narratives or symbolic capital of nation-state political structures have a stake in fostering national identity and culture as synonymous. While cultures can be constructed as intersecting with nationalist characteristics, they are not necessarily bound, though demonstrably it is in the interest of the political structure to present the nation-state agenda as legitimized by the cultural overlay.

In every case I can think of, nationalist constructions presume to represent a multiplicity of cultures, or discrete communities within their borders. Then, we have cultures that transcend national borders, such as Hip Hop, Coca Cola and the Catholic Church. Finally, we know of instances like the Kurds, with no sovereign homeland occupying territory in at least three separate nations. I suspect one's identity with culture(s) is primarily affective, a powerful set of feelings of convergence with cultural norms and values—what Pierre Bourdieu would call *habitus*. From the point of view of nationalist stakeholders, it is always desirable, and maybe even essential, that the people's feelings and identities align with a national agenda. Lest revolution come calling.

In telescoping fashion, my fourth allegiance is to my extended family; my commitment to my kin is so close to and associated with my cultures that I cannot say a priori which I owe a greater fealty to—kin or culture; it comes down to context, the interstices where identities and circumstances are multiple, fluid, and amorphous.

My final allegiance is to me: *To thine own self be true.* I am valuable. I am important. But not more or less important or valuable than anyone else. And assuredly less valuable and important than any family, community, or culture in the world. Which are, in turn, of less consequence than our speciation. Within one's core community and family is the self, the last entity.

To the extent that self can identify with more than one community and culture; to the extent self can first consider what is in the interest of the species as a whole (instead of one faction or class against another); to the extent self/selves can consider the consequences of this or that policy or pattern of consumption against the litmus of biospheric consequence; this might be considered an ethical standard on which to weigh social relationships, inequalities, and the discourses involved in maintaining or opposing them.

In my working model of hierarchy of identities, note that nowhere is there a category of nation-statehood. I submit the nation-state model, as the latest, most potent example of ethnocentrism, is archaic, obsolete, and dangerous to our mutual sustainability, the human family and the biosphere. We are approaching a population of 7.5 billion humans and everywhere you turn, human pressure impacts ecological niches. The carrying capacities of many ecosystems are either reeling or on the brink of collapse. I contend the major problems we face are not the circumstances or consequences of humans against humans—though that seems to have been our primary focus and the stuff of our histories these millennia. Rather our biggest, most persistent problems today are the results of we humans against the biosphere; our assault on our own Eikos—our 'house'—the planet on which we live.

Ok, it's a little sketchy, I'll admit. And it lacks specificity at culture, community, family, and self levels where the issues of inequality, injustice, and suffering are most apparent, as applied to gender, racial, ethnic, and sexual politics.

Finally, I gave some thought to proposing an over-arching *nous*-sphere, the summation of all interdependent being/ knowledge—then the coffee wore off and I came to my senses; what we don't need is yet another level of abstraction, I suppose…

The *other* Vietnam War

Back in the late 1960s many people, especially younger ones who had a more personal stake in the event, found themselves questioning the American military intervention in Vietnam. The expression "My country, right or wrong" came under increasing scrutiny. One result was the realization that the government was not just a distant, Big Brother-like behemoth demanding absolute fealty, but was, in fact, an extension of *We the people.* We believed that if we were willing to take responsibility for the Leviathan of our collective creation, this destructive course could be slowed and eventually diverted, provided enough people, energy, and influence could be enlisted. "Participatory democracy" became the watchword.

Although our government was sometimes aloof and intractable, and was often the handmaiden of industries whose interests ran counter to those of most Americans (to say nothing of SE Asians), nevertheless we believed, perhaps naively, that it was not impervious. We could make a difference.

It was as if the poet Yeats wrote for *our* generation when he penned in *The Second Coming*, "…the blood-dimmed tide is loosed, and everywhere/ the ceremony of innocence is drowned." I was unable to say, in continuing the poem, whether "the best lack all conviction, while the worst/ are full of passionate intensity." But these were decidedly heady times; the blood was up, and none I considered *my* peers lacked conviction *or* passion to match.

I became involved ("radicalized" was the popular term of the day) in February 1967, *long* before it was acceptable in Tucson, AZ, to publicly oppose US foreign policy. At first a handful of us picketed the downtown post office, i.e., the local "Federal Building," one afternoon a week to fairly overt hostility: taunts, jeers and ridicule but not outright brickbats. This was soon followed by my public renunciation of the Selective Service System—that branch of the military responsible for the often-unwilling conscription of disproportionately poor, rural, undereducated minorities—to a rather large campus audience, the media prominently in attendance. And for a time I was a spokesperson on campus representing the opposition, when a military recruiter was invited to address a fraternity or other such groups.

Then, as a kind of culmination to my radical career, in December of that year I participated in a sit-in. This occurred on the day the Tucson army inductees were to be transported to a military base to begin basic training. Only, in my case, *stand-in* would be more accurate; while several of my comrades crouched in a huddle in front of the large Greyhound-like bus, I stood near its front acutely mindful of the driver revving the engine. To be sure, my sympathies were with the Resistance, and I was there to make my voice heard (the sign I held encapsulated my sentiments rather well, I thought: *War is the enemy, not people*). But I was damn sure my statement didn't extend to my mangled corpse under a giant wheel of that bus! I was prepared to leap to the side at the slightest forward movement; passions ran high on *both* sides and even then, there was essentially no middle ground. Within minutes, of course, the police appeared and rousted our meager band out of the path of the bus, which was soon on its appointed way.

Some days later two FBI agents appeared at my door; it turns out that by standing, I was perhaps the most conspicuous among the group, the most "photogenic" for the evening news, and certainly one of the more easily identifiable (not that inconspicuousness was aspired to). I was the first of several tried for malicious mischief, unlawful assembly and disorderly conduct—all misdemeanors—and found guilty on two of the three counts, in the spring of 1968. Ramifications of the Vietnam War were not permitted to be introduced in the trial. As I had had a clean record, I was given a suspended sentence with three years' probation.

It is common knowledge nowadays that the Vietnam War was heretofore our nation's most unpopular conflict; also that the will of the people had shifted over time until our stated goals, our rationale for fighting there were no longer credible or tenable. It is still worth noting, however, that while the war officially ended in the spring of 1975 to near-universal relief, in the winter of 1967/spring of 1968 it was a very different story, indeed.

And parenthetically, I *do* concede justification for honoring our brave young men and women who fought and, in many cases died, because their nation called. But you know, it rankles that we still lack the will to honor those who stood *against* that "blood-dimmed tide" seven, eight years before its belated conclusion.

(Fall 1996)

Not sown

Not sown
by some premeditating reaper
no consciousness of intent or purpose
passively swaying to an unseen force
as if dancing to inaudible music
with but one limb as anchor
a tiny flower
reflecting the dazzling light
glared back at the sun
dared to face in defiance
until a care
less unyielding mass
in the form of a boot
crushed that insurrection

Time travel: the mind is a dangerous thing

I've been back a few days now; a two-week vacation in Japan culminating with the nearly-5000-mile flight back to Portland. Jetlag, though severe this time, has gradually given way to orientation according to Oregon time. Why did I perceive it a harder physiological adjustment this time? To be sure, I'm getting older, less resilient, and not as used to these long-haul flights as I was in my heyday. For several years I flew the Tokyo-Oregon RT at least once a year (typically in summer) and often flew to other, far-flung destinations as well (e.g., Australia, Bali, China several times, Europe)—all separate trips. But the fact is, the flight *to* Japan was not nearly as grueling (and never has been) as the diurnal/nocturnal adjustment resulting from a flight *to* the US *from* Japan. And an anecdotal poll of my fellow trans-Pacific travelers bears out my experience.

How can this be (*he asks, his fancy piqued*)? I propose this tentative explanation: Flights to Japan originating from the west coast usually leave from late morning to early afternoon arriving in Narita (90 min. out of Tokyo), after 9~10 hours' flight, late afternoon to early evening the following day. Flying the exact same route, *going* takes about an hour longer than *coming*, owing to the jet stream which chugs along at 75~150 mph (depending on whether we're tacking across it or plowing into it headlong) always from west to east, itself a function of the earth's rotation. Commercial jets aren't built to fly *above* the jet stream and some of the stratospheric storms. And to fly *below* the jet stream would be far more dangerous via the mountaintops and tropospheric storms. The best one can hope for regarding the jet stream configuration (because it regularly shifts north and south, despite its steady west-to-east flow) is to tack across it like a schooner into a gale, i.e., using avionics to propel the plane forward while being pushed sideways.

Once in Narita, it's a two hour process through customs and onto NEX—the Narita Express—the fastest means from the airport to downtown Tokyo or Yokohama. They depart every 40 minutes or so. Invariably, "homecoming" is achieved late afternoon/early evening—are you ready?—the *next day!* So you've lost a day; are you with me? During that nine-hour-plus flight you've approximated the arc of a great circle from Seattle to Tokyo and at some point (eight time-zones from the West Coast of the US, PST?) you crossed the International Date Line, the invisible demarcation snaking from the North Pole to the South Pole from which, heading west, a new day commences.

Japan is 16 hours *ahead* of PST. Ergo, leaving Seattle at 1 pm, adding 10 hours for the flight, equals 11 pm *Seattle time.* Add 16 hours to account for the relative longitudinal position and you have an arrival time of about 3 pm Japan local time the following day. By the time you've cleared the bureaucracy and navigated the local transportation the day is shot, despite the fact that it may be only 7 or 8 pm. The trip's been a bit of an ordeal under the best of circumstances, it's pushing 4 am according to your body's clock—well past "Bedtime for Francis." Frankly, having *lost* a day weighs less heavily psycho/sociologically than having plunged (back) into a thoroughly different culture—with but 7 hours' difference from what your body says it is.

Truthfully now, who hasn't "lost" a day, or the better part thereof, at one time or another? Through a *Hutsuka yoi* (hangover), exhaustion, or illness huge chunks if not the whole of a day have simply passed us by while we were unconscious, asleep or otherwise stuporous. It could be likened to not knowing you've missed something because you never "had" it to begin with.

Ah, but the existential costs of traveling the other way! The flights *to* the West Coast depart in late afternoon. Sometimes the flight is delayed and if that occurs during the winter, you can actually experience the sunset on two different continents on the same day... But let's say everything goes as expected and you leave around 5 pm, local time. It's only an 8~8 ½ hour flight in this direction because you've been pushed along by the jet stream. Count an hour for customs, etc., and it's 2 or 2:30 *am* your time; definitely sleepy time.

In Oregon time, however, it's 10:30 am on the *same day!* Your family, friends, and everybody's been up for two or three hours and their day is just getting underway while you're wrung out; you can't help thinking at 10:30 this morning in *your* consciousness—some 16 hours ago—you were putting the final touches to packing your baggage, getting ready to say your goodbyes, and start the transportation process to get to the airport.

So wrap your mind around this: It's not being in two places at the "same" time (though, in the socially recognized sense of time, that is certainly true). It's more like having the same time to live, again, in a different place. I'm pretty comfortable saying that; it has a rational contour to it. But I gotta tell you, in all the times I've made this passage, I've never gotten

114

used to the adjustment *on this leg* of the journey, not going to Tokyo from Portland. Affectively, metabolically, it's a different experience. Somewhat psychedelic, I'd have to say.

Of course, in traveling forth and back across the Pacific one merely restores balance to the time gained/lost ratio (in the Physiological/Cosmological-Time sense), even if the trips are separated by months or years. But to extend the back-to-the-future/on-to-the-past confusion: I've traveled around the world twice in my lifetime—both times traveling *with* the earth's rotation, from West to East. So here's the nut: Am I not two days *younger* than someone of the same birth date who didn't circumnavigate the globe in the West-to-East direction? And *four* days younger than that someone traversing the globe twice in the opposite direction?

The mind reels…

(early Winter 1999)

Gnawing evening

Gnawing evening
hunger. Late pizza
bolted with beer. Now
fretful, sleepless in
the inky swamp of deep
night, come waltz
through the fart-bubbles
with me.

(Fall 1994)

Dialogue with the Devil

Prologue

There is certainly no dearth of literature on Godhood, or Godness, in its many manifestations. God the Father, the Patriarch, the Prime Mover, the All-Seeing Eye, the Holiest of Holies. From the sacred texts—the Bible, Qu'ran, Bhagavad Gita, Torah, Book of Mormon—to subsequent interpretations and critiques, clearly the deity/ies need no further advocacy.

Ah, but the counterpart to the embodiment of goodness, virtue, and light, the requisite foil, the opposite without which goodness, virtue, and light have no meaning—such an entity goes begging. Having gotten short shrift, shafted, blown off, ignored and all but abandoned by reasonably educated and otherwise inquisitive folks. Not getting its due, you might say. But darkness, or at least obscurity, appears to be a part of the human condition; vice and temptation play roles in our lives. If too many of us too often drift toward mediocrity, if not morally compromised/ing behavior, then why shun a legitimate examination of our "darker," more diabolical nature?

On such a basis, I decided to engage my less-than-godlike self (and that of others, I hasten to add) as if it were somesort of an externality, represented as the trope, Satan the tempter, the seducer of humankind's soul—and see where the conversation might transport me. I take as moot whether I'm actually talking to

117

this other being, this *doppelganger*, this complement of myself that presumes to exert power over me, or talking to a sort of alter-ego of myself.

Furthermore, I find that, despite a familiarity with various representations of the Devil over the centuries, I don't gravitate toward or seem to need a particular corporal manifestation to sustain communication; no scarlet-hued, horned-and-tailed, glowering, slavering, yellow-eyed demon is requisite. The depth and breadth of a mind unto itself, disembodied, has the ability to intrigue, stimulate, and to invite response/interaction without the necessity of a body to associate it with. Often age, gender, "ethnicity," and physiological characteristics only serve to distract and codify the Otherness of one's interlocutor. *Ah, but could this be a diabolical feint, a stratagem to disarm me?...*

Dialogue

First off, I want to know how I should address you: Beelzebub? Lucifer? Satan? *Mr.* Satan? Your Badness?

People get too caught up with names in the same way they seize on images or icons. You don't need a name for me; you address me by addressing me. Call me what you want when talking about me, it doesn't matter. But I know when you are talking to me. By the way, that was a pretty astute observation you made about not having to "see" a form of me in order to communicate with me. That gets us off to a good start.

I'm not sure I like the sound of that. But to continue, you don't seem to be omniscient; are you lacking in traditional god-like qualities?

OK, Rule #1: We don't talk about your so-called gods. Perfection of any stripe is certainly not one of my aspirations, and it is notably absent among you humans. I know a thing or two but I'm not omniscient, though if I were you, I wouldn't test me on it. If you ask me, that old fraud you call god has gotten away with murder for far too long by making you gullibles believe he/she/it is all powerful, all knowing, and being in all places at once—while, at the same time, acting on your behalf. Ha!

I suppose your antipathy for the divine is to be expected. So no more talk of god; got it. Then, if there are no other conversational taboos, what is your purpose? What have you got planned for me and my fellow humans? What about the other life forms?

Good question! Not to put too fine a point on it, chaos is my stock-in-trade. Good old-fashioned chaos is pure Hell. Or, on a different level, pure Heaven. But on the level you humans primarily operate on— the presumption of order and control over each other as well as the rest of life on earth, the biosphere— chaos is as hellacious as it gets. I do my bit here and there to lure you mortals into even greater depths of self-indulgence, greed, and avarice, leading inexorably to the corruption and dissolution of your body and your body-politic, the unraveling of the social fabric. You get the picture...

The rest of the flora/fauna I've got no quarrel with. In fact, you could think of me as their advocate, a dedicated activist on their behalf. It's YOU who are the blight. Such species solipsism had never been seen before you; no other life form (above the microbial level) had acted on the credo, "We are the center of the universe; we are its purpose. We want Bigger, Better, Faster, More!" and been so wantonly profligate as a result. Since you've made such a big impression, it's unlikely your ilk, once you're gone, will be seen around these parts for another several hundred million years. In an unprecedented act of cooperation, the surviving species will see to it. In other scenarios, scattered, small enclaves survive and begin to recapitulate human evolution; a kind of Dawn of Civilization, Part II. Which could get a bit tedious so, and you're not to take this personally, I've got my money on outright human extinction.

Isn't that a little harsh? I mean, we humans have created some good things as well as bad, haven't we? Nowadays we consciously protect habitats, and even restore some species and their habitats to viable ecosystems.

Excuse me while I sneer; "restore some species and habitats," my arse! You should listen to yourself: full of smug self-importance. In some very limited instances you have made paltry gestures at preventing the extinction of a few dozen species, high-profile token exceptions that, in every case, were driven to the brink by human incursion in the first place. Meanwhile, in virtually every habitat, every niche around the earth, interdependent species are in full rout and vast skeins of life are teetering on the brink of complete unravel. Thus, if we are to continue this conversation, you're going to need to be more honest with the motives, means, and the consequences of your species' conduct. So, by all means, do come forth! What kind of "good things" were you offering in mitigation? What evidence have you that might redeem your species?

Ouch! No need to be rude about this. I guess you would say that our great deeds are really the ways we've leveraged the environment to enhance our lives. I'm beginning to see that our species-centric viewpoint permits, and even encourages, us to believe in our primacy/superiority, in parallel with the Christian tenet that we have been created in the image of God the Father, destined to have dominion over all other creatures.

Hey, last warning! Watch it with the god stuff! If being what you call rude is what it takes to shake you out of your lethargy/complacency and into recognition of your folly, it's the least I can do— believe me! I admit, I'd be out of a job if the insight of your species-centrism got disseminated, and remedial action were immediately introduced in deference to the rest of the biosphere. Of course, that would entail you humans reversing course in most of the trends of resource extraction and patterns of consumption— yeah, that'll happen. As you say, when pigs fly.

But even if all this really is unfolding and not just a sociopathic delusion of your febrile mind, who's going to put any credence in what you've got to say? You're not even close to the mainstream of your social narrative, am I right? Most of your people take you to be a bit of a crackpot? I thought so! I may be unemployed when you misnamed Homo sapiens (Man the wise, *snort!*) self-destruct. But in that event, I won't mind retiring. In the meantime I suspect there are still plenty of chances to muck up the works. Or more accurately, help you muck up the works.

Your suggestion of my occupying several degrees' distance from the habitus of my national identity, the dominant narrative, is very prescient. And humankind's predilection to muck up the works, as you put it, is certainly not new. But I can only cope with aspects of our collective folly in finite doses with breaks in between. Consider this change of subject such a break...

I'm a little surprised you're so accessible. I would have thought you were far too devious and mysterious to talk to mere mortals—but maybe that's an aspect of your deviousness. You must know my soul is already "damned," according to the Christians, having forsworn Christ as my personal savior. Thus, no motive to lure me away from a "fold" I'm not a member of.

Hell, that may be true; it's not for me to say whether you are damned or not. The thing is, I'll talk to anybody who'll initiate the communication. It's just that most folks are too cowed to even consider the interaction. Too intimidated to risk their "immortal soul" on a little honest colloquy. However, in your language the record shows a few brave and curious enough to engage me; Mark Twain and Ambrose Bierce come to mind. Of course, the Germans have Nietzsche and Goethe (*Faust*). The Brits have Bertrand Russell, and these days, Richard Dawkins and Mick Jagger....

Thank you, I think. For associating me with those titans of artistic expression. So, if you will, tell me something about yourself; how did you come to be who/what you are? What is the source of your power?

I won't be talking much about myself or my trade. It's better if we keep this conversation impersonal; as much as we can, in the realm of ideas. Again, it benefits us little by fixating on physiological aspects instead of (or even in addition to) the quality of our thoughts, as expressed in our statements. Power is a relative and transitory thing, even for me. My power over humans is hugely overrated. Needless to say, I get blamed all the time. For example, in your lapses of libido, and other craven lusts: "The Devil made me do it!"

Ok, back to your goal of complete social collapse: How are you going to orchestrate it? Or help us bring it about, if you'd rather?

It ought to be obvious that prolonged concentration of power in the hands of the very few, allowing these few to dictate the terms of polity, is a recipe for systemic inequality and institutionalized elitism. Meanwhile, the decades, even centuries, reel off with this paradigm well-understood and token movement toward, if not outright retreat from, socio-economic parity. Perhaps the rapid decline and ultimate collapse of the petroleum economy will trigger the lurch into the abyss. Or perhaps global climate change will precipitate the collapse of some key life forms (the oceans' plankton?), creating a domino effect up the food chain. Then there's always the possibility of some nasty little pathogen (H5N1? MRSA?) lurking in the shadows, patiently mutating, waiting to pounce, to wreak pandemonium the likes of which could dwarf the influenza pandemic of 1918~'19. Count on it; one way or another, a lot of people will get the opportunity to prove their mettle. We've got exciting times ahead!

Are you saying you don't know the outcome? Could humanity reverse this trend, or experience a so-called soft landing?

I do not know the outcome, and I certainly don't accept that it is preordained. But your own leading indicators have told the story for all who cared to look. It's basic economics—and physics as well. You can't continue to base an economy, and expect it to expand and prosper, on the extraction of finite resources, petroleum as prime example. In the last century, you became increasingly dependent on it, knowing for decades that the end was predictable. Furthermore, the intersection of the trajectory of increasing global demand with the one of shrinking supply is bound to launch spiraling inflation, followed by political/ economic collapse. At that point, the monetary system gets renegotiated on a local basis. It would be good, in this scenario, if you had skills associated with small-scale, *un*mechanized agriculture and live in a place where this were possible. Or have some other necessary skill(s) worth trading grain for. I could go on. But what's your interest; you looking to be the next Adam?

NOOoo, thank you! I'm an old man and I just might, with luck, slide on out prior to the feces hitting the air-circulation device. My interest is curiosity about the ultimate status of my species, in your view. Despite the manifestly immoral acts we have committed/ are committing against each other and the remaining biosphere, despite it all, I'm having a hard time conceding we humans have amounted to little more than an extreme burden on the rest of our fellow creatures—excepting pigeons, crows, mosquitoes, rats, and cockroaches, I suppose. I don't mind admitting I'm attached to my human family, flaws and all.

You like what you intuitively recognize to be your kin: your fellow beings. It's your primary identity, no surprise there; it's hard-wired, after all. But being attached to your human family doesn't let you off the hook from the epic calamities you humans have wrought. Then, in addition to your human family, there's your connection to your American family—history's all-time greatest scourge. You personally, and you collectively, must answer for that. The privileged and elitist managers of your nation-state identity have coaxed credulity and acceptance of the myth of a representative democracy for over 200 years. But now, in the dawn of the 21st century, it is no longer possible to maintain the sham. From the global to the domestic scale, America's follies cry out for expiation. As a participant, why don't you elaborate some of your follies, Cassandra?

Wait, are you calling me Cassandra? That's a woman's name; I'm a man!

Ha! Have you forgotten we both agreed to the advantages of a disembodied dialogue? Here, in the Nousphere? Relax, it's just a name I refer to you.

You know, I think I am better off taking lumps for my own transgressions, my own bona fide fuckups, and not try to advocate for the national entity I was born into, let alone the sins of all mankind. By the time we've trotted out the lot I've personally earned, and poked and prodded them awhile, that might be all I'm good for. The being we've come to know might, by that time, have taken such a psychic drubbing for his follies that he's no longer willing or able to get his hackles up over yet another accretion of human folly.

Not so fast: Will you admit to John Donne's aphorism: *No man is an island*? While it is technically possible to live in complete isolation from other humans (beyond the early years), will you acknowledge that such a life would have little meaning for you? That you need people to make life meaningful?

I do so acknowledge.

I thought as much. If you are an interpretation of the interaction with your environment, human and otherwise, you don't get to slither out; you are dammed to the extent your social context is dammed. Sum totally, you late-20th/ early-21st Century humans are the most indulgent, wasteful, and destructive species since the beginning of life on earth. And the most ruinously profligate subset of humans are you citizens of the United States of America. That's strike one for being human and strike two for being American! Despite neither of them being your choice, there is some serious atonement due. None but a fool would assert that life is fair. Still, I recognize that you really aren't all alike. And that the difference has precious little to do with race, gender, age, status, or ethnic orientation, and very much to do with a sense of shared stewardship. That some of you in varying degrees actually mitigate some of the damage of the others, albeit too little too late. Fighting the noble but futile cause. Pissing in the wind.

Hey, you're creeping me out. I'd like to quit this conversation for the time being, step back, and ruminate over some of this. Is that ok with you? Will it be possible to resume at another time?

I'm afraid I can't take credit for your emotional state, which in this case, derives from the sudden and brutal denouement of your complicity in the destruction around you. Nonetheless, I remain at your service, in a manner of speaking. Take all the time you need. I've got eons. Do get back in touch whenever you're in the mood. Pleasant dreams...

Epilogue

Was I getting drawn in? Did I extract myself in the nick of time? I don't know. At no time did I feel any more imperiled by this communication than, say, driving on the Sunset Highway during rush hours. At this point, I don't think I could say with any certainty whether I was playing with my own satanic fantasies or somehow managing to channel the Evil One, Itself—in some ways seeming to struggle with the responsibility of maintaining reputation.

I'm still grappling with this final comment:

I don't traffic in redemption, and that's a fundamental dilemma for you humans. The hard work of doing "good" while not knowing if it's going to make a difference—to you at death (for those laboring under the illusion of an afterlife), to your community, and to the earth. Can you make a difference? Will it matter? Because you often need to believe that a Better World, however defined, is achievable just to keep from losing all hope or purpose. Well, it's true that the ultimate consequences of your deeds are ultimately unknowable. You can never know if your effort is "worth it." But what else have you got?

(Summer 2005)

In the beginning

In the beginning was the
   one for the money
on the second day he created
   two for the show
on the third day he ascended into
   three to get ready
and be
   fore you know
It, the undertaker

A modest proposal

It is hard for me to take pride in America these months, years. While my moral compass compelled me to oppose America's invasion of Iraq from before its inception, it was sometime later that I concluded the best solution to our post-invasion debacle was to begin an *immediate* military withdrawal. But for a long time, I was troubled by the recurring, somewhat standardized argument as to why US forces should remain, summed up by a metaphor cited by a Senator adopting the Pottery Barn Ethos: *If you break it, you own it.*

A problem with the metaphor is that a ceramic item is either whole or broken; the event that renders it broken from whole (always in this direction, following the law of entropy) occurs all at once. Whereas the somewhat-arbitrarily bounded nation-state, Iraq, with its 24+ million people comprising at least three distinct ethnic groups "breaks" in stages, shatters in agonizing pieces of human tragedy on a daily basis. If Iraq has descended into internecine fighting despite our best efforts to maintain control and stabilize the society; if we continue to kill and wound innocent civilians (being killed/ wounded in the process); if our chief function as occupiers is to serve as a unifying target for all the factions, then it's time to declare *Mission accomplished* (again!) and leave.

But we do bear responsibility for the chaos and destruction we've unleashed, so it's incumbent on us to try to mitigate the bloodshed upon our leave-taking. To that end, I propose that America commit to the following three conditions by way of securing/stabilizing the area we have "broken," and to restoring some credibility in the global community.

1) We agree to pay reparations. For starters, reconstruction of Iraq's infrastructure should enhance prospects of social/political stability.

2) We offer up former-President George W. Bush and key members of his administration to the World Court for war crimes and whatever additional international crimes that may be appropriate.

3) We place US forces in the Middle East under United Nations command. Though it is likely that Iraqis will speak with one voice opposing further American involvement in that blighted country, we need to legitimize the UN as the sole global forum for coping with large-scale inter- (*and* intra-) national conflict.

Can you spell S-u-d-a-n?

(an unpublished Letter to the Editor, *The Oregonian*, Fall 2004)

Waiting

He was waiting and I saw him there
waiting and idly watching the shadow creep
away from the tree he sat beneath.

He seemed to be waiting for something,
purposeful, so I asked him what he thought
but he didn't know or care
enough to want the connection

while the shadow bolted to the horizon

(Prescott, AZ 1963)

A bookstore coffee shop: an interpretation

Friday morning, 11:45 AM: Inside the perimeter of a coffee outlet, itself inside a nationwide book retailer, in an urban mall in PDX. Seated at a small table with a *house coffee*, the cheapest caffeinated fare offered: 12 oz. Of steaming, black coffee at $1.50. Even though my order was not "to go," it was served to me in a cardboard cup with a molded plastic top and a ruffled cardboard sleeve to protect my fingers from getting burned. A large, vertical cooler filled with bottles of fruit drink and bottled water stands eight feet in front of me. Next to it, running 12 feet to the cash register, is a food display counter with far more (in variety *and* shelf space) discreetly lit dessert offerings than sandwich-like, nutritious fare (mark up higher on sweets? Pandering to the public's baser tastes? Seducing the captive customer as s/he stands waiting to pay the fare?).

12 to 15 people seated at these 24"-diameter tables around the semi-enclosure roughly half and half singles and pairs. Four more queued up at the cashier. Just now two elderly women are waiting on service, money in hand. Drinks provided, they move slowly, showing extra care in navigating unfamiliar terrain, toward a place to sit.

Transactions at the cash register are the only conversations within earshot and even these are sketchy. These transactions, these product/service money exchanges, are perfunctory; it's a busy-enough time so everyone has sufficient sociolectic awareness to minimize the small talk. It currently takes three minutes from entering the line to picking up one's order.

Affective considerations: 1) Lighting: diffuse, adequate, and unobtrusive. 2) Temperature: estimated in the high 60s; comfortable to me. 3) Aural field: music just loud enough to hear, not loud enough to hold one's attention. Folk-rock genre. 4) Sensory field: Coffee is hot, but not scalding hot, possessing a rich flavor, and not bitter; cheap and efficient free-standing chairs with molded-plastic seats and backs make for moderately comfortable seating—for 20~30 minutes. 5) Visual field: unremarkable, probably by design. Set apart from the bookstore with a low barricade covered in faux plants. A superficially pleasing place to sit and wile away a few minutes.

Now, if only a neon-highlighted chocolate mousse in the glass case hadn't started beckoning, whispering my name…

(Qualitative Analysis class assignment, Winter 2003)

Part Three

Grackle and the environment

So let's say, for the sake of discussion, that all those Chicken Little—*The sky is falling, the sky is falling!*—geo-climatologists are wrong in their projections of drastic climate change as a result of human generation of carbon dioxide and other greenhouse gasses. Wrong in their projections of disruptive-but-survivable oscillations of climate instability at roughly 350 ppm CO_2 in our atmosphere—while we currently have 390-plus ppm and climbing! Natural fluctuations of CO_2 in the atmosphere have, indeed, occurred for millions of years, long before human tenure; no change so drastic in the last two million years, however. Of course trying to look into the future is always fraught with the likelihood of some degree of error. Too much emphasis placed on one attribute, while too little recognition on another. Grackle understood that our human capacity to imagine different possibilities was amazing and wonderful; it was nonetheless quite limited. The more into the future and/or the more detailed the projection, the more apt to be error prone.

Given that our estimates of the future are not likely to come wholly true, Grackle reasoned, a little risk assessment was in order. Our behavior will generate one of two possible outcomes, in regards to the CO_2/climate-change debate. We, collectively, could continue our current course of fossil-fuel consumption, or we could launch into drastic curtailment.

139

Consider the assertion, *There is a direct connection between climate change run amuck and human use of fossil fuels.*

A) If the statement turns out to be false, say, in a decade from now, but in the meantime we've acted to minimize our fossil fuel intake, and our CO_2, NO_2, etc., discharge, what have we lost? Such a transformation would require radical reorientation of energy generation, and be expensive, *but* will ultimately be required anyway. Any adjustment in the direction of making us live more sustainably is to the good, even if it happens faster than it would absolutely have to happen. It would be hard to call that potential "error" in anticipation a mistake of serious consequence. We'd be apt to clap ourselves on the shoulder and laugh at what *nervous Nellies* we'd been.

B) On the other hand, if the statement is even more obvious ten years from now, but we rolled the dice and continued the party, gorging on petroleum, coal and natural gas—as if there were no tomorrow, ha!—the consequences are almost sure to be even more dire. We will have compromised the ability of future generations to live in circumstances even remotely like the one we treat as our entitlement. We'll be sorely wishing we could have the Nellies' outcome.

If one were going to err to some extent (and let's be honest, we *Homo sapiens* have been known to screw up on occasion), then wouldn't it be prudent to err on the side of caution? Humans could launch into mitigation and begin to rein in fossil fuel usage, *just in case,* and relatively minimal social upheaval need take place.

> *The evil that is in the world always comes of ignorance, and good intentions may do as much harm as malevolence, if they lack understanding. On the whole, men are more good than bad... but they are more or less ignorant, and it is this that we call vice or virtue; the most incorrigible vice being that of an ignorance that fancies it knows everything...*

Albert Camus, *The Plague*

How could one not be demoralized recognizing this paradigm—and seeing the choice Grackle's co-inhabitants continue to make? Begging the question, which attitude toward perceived "reality" is most conducive to future social wellbeing, if not outright survival?

Ah, but in the here-and-now, one is far more apt to feel welcomed by adherents of the dominant narrative to the extent s/he can adopt, or at least play an obsequious public role, a sense of superficial optimism. Assumptions of entitlement, interpreted as continued social development, hand in hand with technological advancement are required, of course. One is expected to express optimism for renewed "business as usual"—steady growth and a return of consumer confidence—and you are a back-thumped, high-fived member of the fold.

But woe betide the messenger of an "alternative" future. The source of ill wind, s/he who has the temerity to challenge the happy talk generally will not be engaged, or held accountable for such dire future projections, which is a true pity, as participants from all sides would surely gain from the dialogue. No, the bearer of this "bad" news, never mind the validity of the alarm, is simply banished from social discourse for all but the most banal of interactions. Said person possesses some sort of psychic plague, which is highly contagious and is apt to corrupt hapless (but God fearing and sincere!) folks who are apt to engage him in doctrines of "faith," say, or problems associated with humanity's addiction to fossil fuels as a distant horizon, with lots of time, *decades*, for the next technological miracle to come to the rescue. Meanwhile the population continues to increase, 7.4 billion of us and counting… Like a runaway pathogen, killing its host. Like cancer.

Grackle was able to suspend private thoughts of anarchy and mayhem for snatches of time here and there when social opportunities presented themselves. "Heart-to-heart" interactions were becoming rare occurrences, events to be cultivated, even if, perhaps *especially* if, the interlocutor were of a different socio-politico-philosophic orientation than his. Honestly engaged, such conversations provided hours, days, even weeks of slow follow-up rumination, often yielding insights as to motivations and underlying assumptions.

But such heart-to-hearts were pitifully meager fare, and provided no unexamined data set or overlooked models of how humanity could continue to "grow," knowing sustainability limits were being breached at every turn. There simply were no hopeful and uplifting data sources about future prospects. Grackle had ample opportunity to consider the ancient Greek notion of *hubris*, the overweening confidence and pride that it is humankind's destiny to master/dominate the earth and nature and all that entails—just like it says in Genesis.

He remembered the first time he'd heard the term "doomer," in this case, applied to him by a kindred soul. He had recoiled in distaste. However, in the hours and days since, Grackle had the chance to mull the notion over more than a few times. Despite its stark over-simplification, it's hard to fault its basic characterization. People who adopt this set of assumptions, a world view that more-or-less corresponds to Pisswing's, are straight-up *doomers*. Over time, he came to own the designation the way an LGBT owns "queer," and Blacks sometimes own "nigger." So Grackle was an unabashed doomer; what did that make the people who bought the happy talk from the fossil fuel industry?

Archetypes such as Prometheus, Icarus, and Pandora, in their unique ways were trapped by their desire to know *more.* Since Adam and Eve in the Garden of Eden, attempting to know *too much* has been said to be humankind's fatal flaw. How could this Abrahamic God give us the ability to think deeply about things, to plumb the deepest recesses of psychic awareness—and then command us *not* to think about certain things? Grackle wondered. He didn't, and perhaps couldn't, believe in such a God. To Grackle, this God looked more and more like a construction created by humans to fulfill distinctly human needs.

We humans have a strong desire to believe in a sense of order, if not justice. If a God created all this, how is it possible this Creator is so indifferent to the plights of humankind, said to be created in His image and destined to have dominion over the rest of life on earth? If He's God the Father and we're His ignoramus, scarcely-more-than-troglodytes-in-suits creation, if

143

we are not provided any more guidance on how to manage our growth in balance with nature than the Bible, we must be 24-hour Reality TV for Him. Continuous episodes on all the amusing ways we humans self-destruct...

These brooding preoccupations must be contrasted by the commonplace expectation of Grackle's co-inhabitants (*exempli gratia*: Hercules Aphid) that science, via its application, technology, has come to humanity's rescue *every time*, certainly over the last century and a half. There was simply no reason to doubt our collective ability to find solutions to this set of global "problems." For one to have doubts about our upcoming technological salvation takes on the resonance of Al Gore's *inconvenient truth*. And on cue, emerges the anti-intellectualism of mainstream America, the deep suspicion and hostility directed toward people who dare to call into question America's exceptionalism, our unique and God-bestowed power and "mandate" to lead the rest of the world... a kind of revised and expanded Monroe Doctrine.

The list is quite long of examples in refutation of the conception of our "unique" characteristics and responsibilities. For current times a partial accounting might well start with misplaced goals and methodology of American military presence in the Middle East, which has created generations of enemies, along with a few sycophant clients. Which illustrates that it is time to rein in military spending, and conduct a strict interrogation of the underlying assumptions of *Pax Americana*'s policing the world. There is the failure to enact some WPA/CCC-like public works (*Socialism!*) to put the country back to work. The lack of courage to enact a single-payer health care system. Continuing to pander to Big Oil, instead of drastically reducing fossil fuel consumption; find the public will to reduce this dependence at a rate of 10% per year—if we have a hope to rein in climate havoc from greenhouse gases for the ensuing centuries, in all probability!

Crazy talk, because all this flies in the face of a mainstream America unwilling to see. All such gaps between what might be and what isn't/or likely soon to be were a bring-down to Grackle. He frequently and spontaneously ran loops through his mind on considerations of desired scenarios and outcomes, and plausible means to accomplish these outcomes—in contrast to the likely consequences of current trends and policies.

Myths/superstitions in circulation since the dawn of human social awareness served creatively and admirably to account for and explain phenomena in the natural world. Meanwhile, empirical knowledge of our physical world, accruing slowly over the millennia, has yielded applications that enhance comfort, health, convenience, longevity, mobility, safety, and in short, an increasing ability to accomplish more with less human muscle energy. For thousands of years, in lieu of human effort in lifting, carrying and pulling weight, ships with wind-driven sails were as good as it got. That and domesticated animal muscle power. The advent of the steam engine in the early-19th century, specifically the coal fired, and later the petroleum and natural gas powered engines, permitted a quantum leap in work performed. We've been on that gravy train ever since.

Currently, our understanding of the basic physics and chemistry, biology and climatology of the world, while not comprehensive, is a number of magnitudes more complete and empowering than that of our primitive ancestors. Yet vast numbers of the human family continue to hang onto these ancient stories as if they represented the best explanation of not only how the earth came to be, but more critically, how we should live accordingly. Such blind obsequiousness to no-longer appropriate or applicable fairy tales would no doubt please our distant forefathers, but are palpably becoming instruments of our folly, and are self-defeating.

Not only are critical portions of the biosphere imperiled through sheer human overpopulation and pressure on increasingly fragile habitats, but human-driven climate change consequences are forcing choices as to which groups of people will survive—assuming in the end, some will—while others will perish. How many people are to be hurled into the abyss, in order to grasp at, to prop up these tired and desperate beliefs?

Anyone with similar gloomy perceptions, while maintaining some respect and admiration for human "accomplishments," would quite rightly feel pangs of sorrow, rage, and a deep miasma of prolonged funk. Such was our boy's plight: What was to be done?

In Grackle's case, this quality of admiration, love, and respect for his species was not limited to but coalesced around and distilled in music. For him, music was the crowning achievement of humankind. How can that be?, the reader asks. What about Love, arguably the greatest expression of the unity of our identity with something, or someone outside ourselves? Grackle could conceive no more pure an expression of that love—and pain, and beauty, and mystery, and anguish, and humor, and sublime peace—save through music. Literature? Bleh! Mere words, sometimes artfully strung together, always compelling the reader to follow along in an attempt to approximate and interpret the writer's mood and imagination.

Music, without lyrics, avoids language-based cognition, or intellectual pursuit; it communicates directly with the psyche. It need not have "meaning" in the sense of a semantic codification, while maintaining the ability to infuse you with awakened feelings. Architecture, graphic arts, applied sciences, dramatic arts, experiments in social organization, you name it, all have contributed enormously to human identity and wellbeing, to be sure. And all pale in comparison to music. If there is an extrinsic godhead, then she/he/it speaks to us, and inspires us most directly and purely through the medium of music. Or so Grackle would have us believe.

Ironically, and thoroughly regrettably, Pisswing had no training in music theory, or experience at playing an instrument, or even reading music, despite his unconscious disposition to seek out and immerse himself in music of any stripe. This text, this written form, is his communication of second choice, the organization of Words, because, simply put, Grackle lacked the ability to make music. Be that as it may, this narrative comprises Grackle's *cadenza* in the ongoing human symphony. It comprises Grackle's brief solo, in themes that are both consistent with the overall symphonic structure, and yet the desire to express his own unique voice and style.

As a personal and temporary solace from the whirling madness he encountered at many a public turn, Grackle would often cloister himself in his den and dip into his extensive music library. An hour or three getting washed in soothing, pulsing waves of music could not help but relieve, if by no other means than distraction, the frustration, anxiety, and the edge of futility, borne by one of Grackle's outlook. A couple-hour musical *bath*—often an eclectic mix of, say, a Mozart piano or a Hayden cello concerto, then literally anything by blues/rock guitar maestro Joe Bonamassa, before settling in with some Paul Desmond/Gerry Mulligan jazz, maybe Miles Davis, or early Billie Holiday—did wonders to his disposition. Often as not, a resolution or accommodation to a minor current dilemma would be forthcoming through virtually no conscious effort. Suggesting music had the ability to "permit" the brain to *play* sufficiently that it could work on the more important imbroglios unencumbered by the omni-directional, nearly omnipresent attention to social connections and obligations in everyday routines. In any event, music was the tonic for Grackle, the balm. It was his ticket to ride, and ride it he did.

On one such Coltrane-induced musical flight of fancy, Grackle caught himself musing on his reptile dysfunction (or *RD*). Truth to tell, it was becoming increasingly difficult to command any respect from his snake. It was as if, after seven decades of intimate association where the relationship was well understood, Mr. Snake had cultivated a mind of his own and was now outright disobeying orders. In his younger, more hormonally charged manhood Grackle would sometimes experience Snakey's disobedience as unwilled and unwanted impetuousness, an immodest and over-eager presentation. But this recent dilemma Grackle found himself in the midst of was rather of the opposite sort. The mind of the host was no longer sufficient to will the body's compliance, further evidence that entropy was asserting itself in a personal way. *The ends cannot hold...*

Perhaps life in idealized form would be ascendant right up to the point of death. Whereas in most cases in Grackle's experience, various peaks were reached at points along the way with considerable *de*scendance in evidence thereafter. Since it is a given that life inevitably gives way to non-life, how much energy and attention was to be employed in extending life, in its diminishing capacities? That was the operative question. In some cases this amounted to stretching longevity when self-awareness is gone. Postponing the inevitable into true absurdity.

To be sure, we should acknowledge our gratitude for the fact that we've survived as long and "successfully" as we have, when so many others have died so much younger. The deterioration, with age, of the various biochemical systems that interact to sustain life is pretty much *the* truism: Life begins, it flourishes—if conditions are favorable—and it ends. It's the other side of the coin. Often as not among the enfeebled elderly, all it takes is a big hiccup in one of those systems and the rest flop over like dominos. It is clear that deterioration is part of the process of shutting down. The alternative is sudden collapse.

He was acquainted with associates, roughly his peers in age, who went to extraordinary means to stretch out/prolong life: walking miles a day, spending hours a day in the gym attempting to tone flaccid muscles, swallowing handfuls of potions and elixirs, pursuing fads that promise longer life. *Ponce de Leon, where is thy Fountain?* Given Grackle's fatalistic frame of mind, he was inclined to be rather minimalist in attending to life's extension. Thus far, though he was not eager to hasten the end, neither was he particularly vigorous in devoting attention to the regimens and devices that promised life's extension. The older he got the more obvious the shrinkage, the diminution, the slackening of his faculties—this in itself was sufficient to moderate his enthusiasm for extending life.

Don't ask what any of that has to do with the soulful, wrenching, plaintive minor-key saxophone probes of John Coltrane. Grackle couldn't tell you.

The famous biologist Edward O. Wilson postulated an emergent consciousness, a *eu*social evolution, whereby people acted principally out of consideration of what was best for the community and the biosphere as a whole—and *not* directly, or specifically in their own self-interest. This would seem to be a contradiction of all we have learned as humans in the latter part of the 20th/early decades of the 21st centuries. The scientific method, discovery and analysis of Self, and thence, recognition of separation and isolation, and the brutal competition inherent in free market capitalism goad us to greater feats of self-aggrandizement. Thus, the number of people who identify with cooperation and *eu*socialization would appear to be minute, but not non-existent. Grounds for hope, perhaps, but not a basis for betting the farm on a quick shift in political will, or anything resembling a widespread social groundswell.

Applied scientific discovery, technology, deserves its due, thank you very much. It has been a pretty big deal in human development for the last three centuries, and *a really* big deal for the last century. Socialization has been the whole ballgame; there is/has been no human development without some social/cultural/lingual unit beyond **extended** family/clan, for how long, **10,000 years**? At least **5,000** years. So how come we're so "good" at technology and so piss-poor at social integration and cooperation with our fellow humans? Significant cultural differentiation and elaboration have been discernible for at least the last 5000 years, while technology, with massive human outcome, has overwhelmingly taken place in the last 150 years. Dynamite, ferroconcrete, antibiotics, electrical and mechanical achievement, mobility and transport powered by fossil fuels: It's an impressive track record, to be sure. Enough of a history to make one complacent about future outcomes. Still, one wonders if civilization as we've known it happened too soon in evolutionary terms. It's been fun, but we haven't exhibited the stewardship to live remotely in balance with the rest of the biosphere.

Balance?! That's just more crazy talk! Behold, we are Humans! Thanks to our unique abilities to innovate technological solutions, we have transcended those antiquated notions of environmental balance. We create our own "environment," so mighty are we. Do other life forms have a hard time making adjustments, keeping up? They must adapt or perish! Extinction happens… Death is not less common than birth.

Stewardship

Sociologically, I occupy the intermediate niche among three living generations. With varying degrees of success, I try to cultivate a close relationship with both my mother *and* my children. (Yes, currently there are four members of the fourth generation. As the eldest is five, my goal is to communicate with the other two generations *on behalf of* this fourth.) Part of that desired closeness entails sharing our identities—i.e., the people, ideas, communities we identify with—and naturally, our notions of our *eikos,* our home, earth, are a piece of that.

My mother, nearly 90, has never had to think of such issues as limits to resources and the human impact on the biosphere until, perhaps, the last decade, so there's no lived experience, no context to allow her to incorporate it into her world view, her frame of reference, her belief system. Since she was born when the total human population was slightly more than a billion, she grew up believing there were virtually no limits to nature's bounty; that the "problems" the environment presented pertained to geographic/ geopolitical obstacles for which hi-tech solutions were in the wings. That had been the case since the Industrial Revolution; she had every confidence of its continuance into the future.

Bless her heart, I can't fault her or her generation for not anticipating/publicizing humanity's collision with a series of biospheric limits. Why should we have expected her generation to see (when they certainly weren't looking for) the coming train wreck? Every generation before her treated nature's bounty as resources to be exploited, all the way back to Genesis and the license from God to rip the biosphere, quite literally, for all it was worth.

By cultural, and maybe universal, tradition parents have commonly expected to pass on to their children prospects of a better life, or at least as good a chance at a decent life as they had. Her generation really did leave their heirs better off than they had had it, especially if you're thinking about the material prosperity of WASP Americans/Canadians in the latter half of the 20th century. No, it really is on our shoulders to foresee and raise the alarm—said calamity is a lot closer now and harder to miss. It's to our generation, baby boomers and a little after (though I'm actually pre-baby boomer, *pre*-WWII), to recognize and try to anticipate the profound consequences of the looming greenhouse-gasses-caused climate shift, converging with the precipitous and accelerating decline of petroleum/natural gas supply relative to demand, all of which is likely to trigger widespread, socio/economic chaos and disaster on the scale of the Biblical Armageddon… *sans* the rapture.

Our generation must bear much of the responsibility for seeing it coming; over decades now, knowing we were over-consuming and not seriously debating it in the public arena. Political and cultural capital, the dominant narrative via the co-opted media, were all stakeholders in the status quo, while *We the people* were not interested in collectively moderating our extravagant indulgences. We have much to answer for.

But here's the rub. Returning to the stewardship theme, part of my obligation to the next generation (to say nothing of quite a few *ostriches* from my own) is to try to gently nudge my fellow humans toward a more balanced, sustainable lifestyle—and pray that in mitigation it's not too little, too late. At this time, virtually all the relevant trends suggest the next generation, as they age, will not enjoy anything like the quality of life that we experienced, as defined by virtually any measure—freedom of global mobility, thanks to profligate consumption of petroleum and natural gas; variety of experiences, plethora of indulgences, along with a largely benign, nominally representative form of government. Again, largely due to economic abundance and prosperity accruing somewhat to the middle class while, of course, mostly to the rich and privileged, basic human rights-cum-freedoms, as well as international conventions, have more or less been tolerated.

When it comes to my children, I know to go very gently; they and I track very different ontological/epistemological premises and orientations. Not wanting to hurt one another, we tread lightly. Nonetheless, over the last several years, I've gotten the distinct impression that pleas for environmental stewardship fall largely on indifferent ears. In bleaker thoughts, I imagine my children, my offspring, *of* me hopefully in meaningful ways, accepting the degradation of the biosphere as harbinger of the Rapture/Second Coming/*Har Magedon.* This passive witness (*if* this is the case) to the human-caused degradation while patiently waiting to be whisked off to Heaven—this image is deeply troubling. Are we just part of earth's widespread species extinction because Our Father has finally lost patience with His wretched human experiment?

After all, there's no mention of the environment, the intricate interdependence of life, in the Bible, that I'm aware of; merely a few references in Genesis to a range of creatures put on earth for humanity's purposes. All of it, ours to exploit. Implying a willfully complicit stance to the impending collapse. Yes, a complicit Father/Creator to all this, but as well a complicit group of people who accept it, unchallenged.

In my bleaker moments, like I said. I feel a little like I'm the microcosm of my species' macrocosm. Some of my generation recognize the predicament and have been more successful in calling attention trans-generationally. In my case, I feel myself the fool for failure to have alerted either my mother or my children to the approaching cataclysm. Shared awareness is shared solution, but my stewardship seems to be wanting.

(Summer 2006)

Which is the way

Which is the way the witches went
why is the answer how
when all you are is all I am
from heretofore unto now

Whence in the margins the angels fled
a measure of meaning unveiled
elusive the question of purpose redressed
whilst o'er edge of the earth we sailed

Towards the outskirts of the interstices
on the fulcrum of the divine
in the axis of the rotation
in the ellipse of love

Oh, what is the nature of night and day
and the locus where hominids dwell
in the notion of whether the weather succumbs
to inverted convolutions most foul

At the pinnacle of happenstance
comes too soon the abyss
nadir, zenith in constant oscillation
'til the bedazzlement of bliss

(Fall 2009)

On being presentable

The little lady wants me to be a notch more dignified; hopes to cultivate in me a modicum of respectability. Can you blame her? She was embarrassed for Akiko, our guest for a recent evening. I'd worn some "Small River" items in my ensemble. The sad truth of it is, half my wardrobe is Small River, i.e., threadbare, snagged, faded, and torn; here and there stained beyond the pale of the deepest cleaning detergent. Each item on its last legs; one short step away from rags—even I admit it.

Ah, but for sheer comfort! And the satisfaction of knowing you're ready for *any* job, be that change a tire, yank noxious vines out of the native flora on Mt Tabor, or digging sod out of the front yard, I'm *ready.* I have no shame: My very most favorite *shirt* (for surely that is what it once was; this much is indisputable) is a dirty-brown checkered cotton number I fished out of the bargain bin for $.99 at the used clothing outlet some five years ago.

She knows I'm educable, but questions my motivation, alas, with some cause. She rightfully points out that my remaining garments are quite socially acceptable. Note that virtually all of this category includes Bettina as a defining agent: Either she gave them to me or was on hand to approve/veto the proposed acquisition.

Coming from Japan, arguably the most fastidiously sensitive/ interpersonally aware culture on the planet, it comes naturally to her, hard wired, as it were, to want her own home and its accoutrements (numbering me, of course) to be neat, tidy, clean, organized, and presentable. Contrasted by my innate predilection toward the unkempt, the slovenly, and conspicuously oblivious to the most basic standards of apparel decency.

What can I say? *Mea culpa.* In my defense, I cite Mark Twain (from the short story, "A Cat-tale"): *"...honest poverty and a conscience torpid through virtuous inaction are more to me than corner lots and praise."*

The poor ol' girl married a *yabanjin*—from the perspective of *the* culture of cleanliness and hygiene, a "barbarian." She got a tough row to hoe.

The environment

I was asked to write a few words about the topic of the environment based on my involvement with the invasive flora in Mt. Tabor Park. The more one thinks about our environment the more complicated it seems. To start with, the term takes on different connotations according to the context to which it is applied. Perhaps the original and most comprehensive usage pertains to the biosphere with its myriads of interdependent species and habitats.

We modern, increasingly urban, hi-tech humans have been so "successful" at constructing or modifying our own desired living space that we tend to use the environment as a backdrop, if not an outright resource for exploitation. We're apt to take for granted the skein on which all life happens. A seemingly minor alteration of the warp here has profound consequences in the woof there. I'd bet our ancestry (before the Industrial Revolution) didn't take nature for granted. Sometimes unpredictable and mysterious in its manifestations, it was—and, of course, still is—the medium that surrounds us like the air we breathe. We don't often think about it, knowing at some level our lives, too, are interwoven with natural patterns. However, dramatic events like recent hurricanes Katrina and Sandy, and the earthquake/tsunami in Fukushima, Japan, serve as grim reminders.

In Mt. Tabor Park, our own neighborhood biological niche, the botanical competition for available ground, water, and sunlight proceeds practically without stop. But the successful flora in this nearly-200-acre "island" must demonstrate considerable resilience to increasing numbers of *the* dominant fauna, us. For example, in the collision between off-trail mountain-bikers and Trilliums, one of the species is devastated while every year there are potentially more mountain-bikers, more downhill "trails." Trilliums could be a kind of "canary in the coalmine," a conspicuous-but-delicate species that signals dire conditions for, perhaps, dozens of other less-conspicuous species. It would be interesting to consider the survival mechanisms of invasive botanicals compared to a native like the Trillium—perhaps a topic for a future article.

Our task would seem to be to preserve where still intact, restore where already trashed, as much of the "natural" habitat as still possible while taking into account the public's reasonable expectation of access to one of the city's showcase parks. Toward that end, the Friends of Mt. Tabor Park promotes monthly service projects March through October, last Saturday of the month, with the cooperation and support of Park staff. At these events, Weed Warriors pursue one or more of the invasive botanicals, trying to hold the line against the handful of species introduced by us that threaten to overwhelm the natives in this beleaguered setting. Come lend a hand! Meet some neighbors, get dirty, and share some camaraderie while making a dent in some nasty ol' Clematis, or English Ivy, and we'll discuss whether said "dent" should be considered Pyrrhic or Sisyphusian in nature.

For information, contact …

Paean to Mt. Tabor,
the commons

If it's not yours or mine
or someone else's it must be
yours and mine and others'—*ours*.
Does that change anything?
Is your relationship to the land
different? One's needed cooperation
with others about the land makes use
very different from this/here be mine,
that/there be yours. It's that ol' trade off
between *get to* and *have to* take more
of a role in our experiment in self-governance.

Get to feels like anticipation, pleasure, desire,
but what on earth is implied by having to do
anything? Compulsion, responsibility.
By what/whom? Constrained by gravity, DNA,
age, gender, the Second Law of Thermodynamics,
to say nothing of a human's limited ability
to comprehend. The realm that we humans
have perhaps the most social influence,
by choice, is negotiating the commons—sharing
in the process of defining meaning and value
in our collective order.

(Summer 2008)

Overpopulation

The Greek conception of cats is, though they may provide some utility to the extent they catch mice, overall they comprise an undesirable parasite of man, and one should do nothing to encourage them. In fact, one frequently sees, usually in the environs of open-air restaurants, feral cats which appear out of sheer hunger appealing for a prospective handout, only to have that person flail out at the wretched creature, doing its best to avoid the kick or the blow. Cats in Greece learn at an early age (or not at all) to be wary of this large, noisy, clumsy beast on which they seem fated to depend.

I eat at the same restaurant maybe twice a week just before work proofreading for the local English-language rag (*The Athens News*). Over time the waiters have accepted me as their bi-weekly foreign curiosity and no longer gawk at me with the avidity of those first few encounters. Two cats seem to have staked out this restaurant as their turf, no matter the active and ongoing campaign to discourage them, and said cats have gotten used to me too. A big, black-and-white-spotted pregnant female and a smaller-but-more-assertive, scrawny gray presumed-offspring of mama cat. They systematically search the under-table areas but warily retreat with the approach of a waiter.

Waiters and busboys are perhaps the feline's worst tormenters. They go on the premise that to treat the animal kindly is only to invite extension/expansion of the problem; that a well-fed cat is not only a likely soon-to-be parent, but is apt to attract its neighbors over for the easy pickings, as well. This attitude would seem to be well founded; surely a straggly alley cat would remember from the outset ("conditioned response," first lesson) where the free meal came from. And just as certainly, it would take but a short interval before the "free" eats were noticed by other *gatoulitzia.* Then, by geometric progression...

Despite all this, understanding the argument, hell, even agreeing, I flaunt the Greek wait-staff at such restaurants. I give all the scraps and inedibles—decidedly more than a Greek would condone (like some boiled, grisly/gristly sheep elbow) to my two rangy dinner guests, fully aware of the implications of my conduct.

Here's the deal: These two cats right here and now are hungry and need to eat to survive. It's not up to me to resolve the cat overpopulation issue; it's not resolvable by one person anyway, though I see my connection. Never mind the distant consequences. I have the means to relieve some of the suffering, even if only for today, and this I do. Starvation can take the day off. There it is: *Aphto einai.*

(Plaka, Athens 1965)

163

On false dichotomies: us vs. them

The problem I have with the "American Dream" is that it excludes, by its singular focus on things American, other groups that have equally valid claims to a dream. Otherwise, it would be something like the *Global* Dream, or the *Human* Dream, wouldn't it? The trap of thinking nationally is getting caught in the duality of Us vs. Them. It's the dilemma of considering all those other countries in contrast to us; in some degree or another, in opposition to us. Anymore, it's a false dichotomy, it seems to me. In terms of securing the survivability of *Homo sapiens* (to say nothing of incalculable numbers of other species), there isn't any *them*. There is only *us*.

Dividing humanity into Americans and non-Americans (or Serbians and non-Serbians, Navajo and everyone else, *ad infinitum*) is a false separation and dangerously empowers nation-states when such entities are archaic and obsolete obstacles to sharing Earth's dwindling resources more equitably, efficiently. If we insist on maintaining the illusion of the old paradigm, the anachronism of nations, or nation-state alliances, bent on dominating their counterparts, or, to put it in the obverse, if we can't or won't learn to cooperate with each other and achieve equilibrium (the recent buzzword, "sustainability") with the rest of the biosphere, we might as well cede ultimate survivability to the Phylum *Arthropoda*, patiently awaiting their chance.

It is incumbent on us humans to bridge the conceptual gap, to make the quantum leap from "My country, right or wrong" and its chauvinist ilk to The Family of Man, complete with infinite variations. Our only international forum, the United Nations, remains the best mechanism we've devised to date to help us work through, and hopefully overcome international conflicts. Superficially or seriously flawed, depending on your political orientation, the UN remains the only vehicle we've got where nations can go to air their differences and be heard by a world body. Better to start, most people would agree, trying to find accord by reasoned dialogue. There will always be time to resort to smart bombs and drone missiles as a last resort.

Some Americans, it is said, are eager to keep the UN hobbled and ineffective. To fully support the UN, the argument goes, would be tantamount to surrendering our sovereignty to strangers, which goes against the Constitution and plays into the hands of our enemies. Fear and conspiracy tend to dominate this world. It is the mindset of the bully who can't bear to surrender his privileged position. The only surviving superpower has a lot to lose, it would seem.

Ethnocentrism, of course, has been a major player in human affairs throughout history. It's safe to say, in fact, that the primary focus of history has been the account of one group's submission to, or triumph over, another. Along with the other driving force in human history, egocentrism, ethnocentrism over the millennia has been a grisly force in alternatively preserving some social structures while destroying others—always at the expense of others.

Are we able to step outside that narrow view; can we raise our collective consciousness to a less belligerent mode of problem solving? Are we capable of thinking/acting inclusively, not exclusively? With proactive meta-cultural discussions nonexistent, and the politics of civilization reactive, slouching toward self-destruction, the arthropods are waiting.

(Fall 1996)

Carlos, the magician

The man stands erect, still,
his back to the attentive onlookers.
There is a hush; with arms outstretched,
poised, invoking the benediction of the deities?
preparing to fly? He raises his body
on the balls of his feet, nods his head,
and brings those two hands, the right one
holding a tapered stick,
through a violent arc, as if boxing
the ears of an errant miscreant.
Suddenly, a thunderous sound explodes
into pleasurable phrases, melodies,
       complementary threads
telling a passionate, non-verbal story.
From a few dramatic gestures Carlos wrings
aural magic: pure feeling
without the mediation of words.
To be sure, Beethoven's authorial contribution
from 210 years ago is dramatic and sublime.
As are the sixty musicians who render the notes
on the page into this precise, coordinated,
       symphonic creation
as per the elicitation of Carlos. A tripartite alloy
for this aural transcendence.

(An *homage* to Carlos Kalmar, Music Director of the
Oregon Symphony, Portland)

167

The Druid working papers

<u>Prologue</u>

My role*: the messenger*

I met an old man while out walking one blustery autumn day. As it happened we were near a small creek, so with hardly a word exchanged beyond the perfunctory small talk at greeting, we passed an idle hour beside that rill listening to the breeze soughing through the sheltering trees and now and then a bird, but mostly the sonorous litany of the water crashing around rocks on its rush to the sea, a few miles distance. I befriended him with a muffin I'd brought from home, and as I was taking leave he passed these pages to me, presented below. He wishes to preserve his anonymity and hence goes by the contrived name of Galen. After several encounters on subsequent occasions—always on chance walks—we became comfortable, if not familiar, in our near-silence with each other. He has agreed to this tentative representation of him.

Lithe and sinewy, he has a full head of snow-white hair and beard. He is gentle spoken, well-educated and well-traveled. Not a doctor, more an alchemist; more metaphysician than physician. Iconoclast of mainstream values and aspirations doesn't begin to tell the story. Being an anarchist at heart, he understands the pitfalls of popularity, if not notoriety, and chooses not to risk exposure. He feels it unwise (rightfully so, I think) to go public, not wanting to draw attention to himself and away from his thesis, which should carry its own weight, and not rely on personality or lifestyle exposition. He declines response to questions of his livelihood, as well as residence. Lastly, he knows well Lord Acton's maxim, *Power corrupts; absolute power corrupts absolutely*, and wishes not to be tempted, in the miniscule chance that any accolades are forthcoming. I have vowed to honor his request for privacy.

Here, then, are Galen's notes.

* * * * *

This is a time between times, one set of assumptions about our place in life giving way to another. People are abandoning the ancient codices, the religious institutions, as less-than-adequate guides to a more complex, multidimensional world. At the same time, there is not yet a sense of meaningful protocol or ceremony to take the place of the old paradigm. People cling to the ceremonies of our Abrahamic religious heritages because they provide a comforting continuity, a way to tap into previous generations. Without such devices, we lose connection with our roots and are cast adrift. Yet much of our fascination with these aspects of ritual lacks commitment, appropriately enough, since the underlying bases for such rituals are no longer relevant to many of the issues we face in the opening chapters of the 21st century. Not that we are now somehow "enlightened"—woefully short of the mark, if judged by no other standard than how we manage to share with each other Gaia's bounty. By contrast to our not-so-distant ancestors, however, we could rightfully be considered well along the path; ready to take the next big step.

In hindsight, our predecessors some 5000 years ago were apt to take such natural phenomena as earthquakes and volcanic eruptions as evidence of angered deities. A solar eclipse could trigger abject terror. For us a rudimentary knowledge of the natural sciences is taken for granted; far from fearing such astronomic events, we can now predict them with great accuracy and travel great distances to witness them. Yet the awe and respect for Nature's array—along with the mystery and magic—have taken a subordinate place to the seductions of infinite electronic distractions. Often as not, we live in urban areas. We march to human-dictated tempos and are occupied by human-centric schedules, such that we become disconnected from the natural rhythms: Sunrise/sunset, moon phases/tides, weather patterns, what the clouds tell us, the equinoxes and solstices. Much has been lost with little to fulfill that need, except the *distractions*.

It is time to begin to establish new ceremonies that affirm our commonality. The poet ee cummings said, "hear ye! The godless are the dull and the dull are the dammed." And we attribute to Socrates, "The unexamined life is not worth living." Life without a spiritual component is a shallow life, indeed.

Let us find new and creative ways to acknowledge the godhead *within* us—to express our affirmation of life and trust in each other, without slavishly fawning before superstitions unworthy of serving us. We need to wrench ourselves from our lethargy. We have too long merely existed, lost in this jaded if not arrogant state, seduced by our comforts and conveniences, our souls not dead but fully benumbed. Consider these, our marching orders.

Credo

Out of a love of wild places and recognition of a need to experience these places alone and in groups in order to preserve our wholeness, I propose we acknowledge our commonality as a loosely knit non-organization, calling ourselves *Druids*. The name is a logical choice inasmuch as the original people we think of as Druids wholly depended on and deeply revered Nature, as evidenced by their animism of the sacred spirits inhabiting all aspects of the world around them. Alas, over the last century or so, we humans' manipulation of many aspects of local environments to our own "benefit" has fed our hubris and allowed us to obscure our dependence on Nature. Which in turn, has led to a loss of respect for the intricate interdependence of all life. The resulting imbalance in our mental well-being can be reduced and mollified by more out-of-doors, out-of-city events as simple as walks.

We all have our personal, independent lives that comprise a necessary part of our identities—the bills must be paid, and furthermore, our egos will not be denied. However, we also have need of community, a common identity. Such a group could help sustain people in the belief that a love of the earth, irrespective (or should I say "disrespective") of its arbitrary political boundaries, is indeed a needful, shared experience.

Taken frivolously, the term could refer to anyone on a casual stroll along the beach, or an excuse for a bunch of people to escape the urban routine for a get-out-of-town excursion. Taken half-seriously, we Druids celebrate a commonality with Nature, tapping, as I believe we do, a collective unconscious theme or purpose in our lives.

Our emphasis, our intent, should be the camaraderie in the shared wonder of Nature in her myriad manifestations. But we shouldn't disavow a need to participate in mainstream politics, using all the tools at our disposal to safeguard our most cherished haunts from greed driven dis-spoilage. As a non-organization, we should agree to remain leaderless and inherently inclusive; what we don't need is another bureaucratic hierarchy with self-important "authorities." Our focus needs to be out of doors, out *There*. Let us bear witness and nurture the mystery and the magic.

Druids, see you in the woods!

(Oregon Coast Range, ca 1983)

In pursuit of harmony: Galen's theology

As in many of the ancient mysteries, in the beginning was Harmony, an intuited sense of belonging in the web of life. Then came the Word (language), mankind's greatest tool, for with it he could symbolize, quantify and evaluate his environment, communicate his perceptions to his fellow humans and thereby share Knowledge. But the terrible price man had to pay for this tool was that as long as he used it for his own ends he would feel separate, and thus would be apart from the Harmony, known by some as *Eden*.

As long as man pits his strength and intelligence against the other species, as well as his fellow man, as long as he strives against that interconnectedness, and toward his own advantage, he pursues an illusion, which is the chief source of his discontent. Within the wonder of humanity's uniqueness we are at once high, exalted, and divine, as well as low, selfish, devious and mean.

How are we to know? Which experience is exalted, which debased? you inquire, not realizing you already have the answer. By this simple fulcrum you may weigh the factors: Does the act, event, or experience expand or contract the universe (or significant subsets thereof)? Is it inclusive or exclusive? Does it promote sharing, or greed and hoarding? Does it suggest we're all in this together, or is it dog-eat-dog, them against us? You need not be servile before another human, but you must neither expect, nor tolerate, servility from another to you.

173

Taken to another level, when we affirm rather than deny, share rather than withhold, we express the Godhead intrinsic within all of us. Conversely, by acting selfishly, out of vengeance, or in mean spirit, we exhibit the metaphoric Demon, which also lurks in us. But here's the important part: We are not merely helpless vessels in which these two antagonists play out their age-old struggle. We have, and it is morally incumbent on us to use, our minds to act on behalf of the positive and hopeful events, and in opposition to the negative, self-serving temptations. It is in such minute steps that we can hope to live full, authentic lives.

With seeming ease

With seeming ease
the breeze
flows coolly about
this transitory projection
that is I.
Found, conquered, surpassed
and soon abandoned
by an ethereal force
that has greater obstacles
to engulf in its course
visiting all, caressing,
it leaves behind in evidence
its contented sigh

(Athens, 1961)

The question of belief

One

  The question of belief is a worthy subject since it seems to underlie so much of our hopes, expectations and orientations. What do you accept on faith? What aspects of your relationship to your fellow humans and the biosphere, beyond all empirical demonstration, drive your beliefs? What gives your life meaning and purpose? By what ethical framework do you evaluate the world? In articulating a response, one need be mindful that ethics entail more than mere human-to-human injustice, discord and strife.

  Any study attempting to recognize, identify, and apply differentiations of the Good from the Bad in life now must include human/biospheric collisions, which ultimately bear far more heavily on the survival of *Homo sapiens* than our petty, perennial, internecine struggles. Even WWII with, what, 60~70 million fatalities, is going to pale by comparison to the "drop off," or species collapse, we humans face (it now seems probable to me) once we trigger any one of several critical sequences. Thus runs one of my more prevalent beliefs *cum* anxieties.

  As an example of how fragile and delicate the interdependent web of life is, what if some combination of 1) abnormal ocean surface temperatures, 2) an unknown threshold of UV exposure, 3) chemical imbalance, and/or 4) pollution "variations" were to cause a local plankton die-off to quickly spread to most of the oceans? Upheavals to the universal provider, bottom of the food chain, are sure to wreak havoc on every form of sea life "above" them, which is to say. all the creatures that feed directly or indirectly on plankton. Even minor collapses can and will ripple into larger waves that become tsunamis.

So what's going on here, an attempt to substantiate details in support of my belief? Yes, surely; why not? If a belief is shared by enough people, if its articulation touches them in enough numbers, their common identity gives them legitimacy to "speak for" a particular point of view, perhaps ultimately, becoming the dominant view within the focus of the belief. By such methods are policies changed to reflect changing public opinions and needs.

Two

A professed Christian once called me an atheist. It shocked me at the time, since I hadn't at all concluded my thoughts on the presence of a deity, one way or the other. It was and remains true that I no longer hold belief in the Christian God, but that by itself did not make me an atheist. She couldn't get away with calling a professed Shintoist, a Muslim, Hindu, or Zoroastrian, atheists since those folks do believe in gods, just not the one she believes in. However, it's true that I don't believe in any of those other institutional deities, either. So does that make me atheist? *Not necessarily!*

As it turns out, I have a deep distrust of codified, doctrinaire, institutionalized belief systems in matters spiritual. I recognize a profound need/desire to celebrate and affirm my however-small-but-conscious part in the biosphere during these few decades I occupy this earthly vessel. Such celebration is often made more meaningful when shared with others, but it is by no means requisite. It can be quite private and personal. A sense of wonder and awe at the web of life can be celebrated in almost any location in almost any manner—the very antithesis of religion. If I may use the terms in such a way, my sense of a "deity" is not monotheistic. I can't think that it's ever a good idea to concentrate all power and control in one being. *Especially* if that being resembled a human!

We could very well in the near future demonstrate *Homo sapiens* to be so clever as to use natural resources and employ ever more sophisticated technology to enhance the lives of proportionally fewer people—but not wise enough, or unwilling, to make enough changes quickly enough to prevent a human-triggered collapse of Armageddon-like proportions—as a direct result of human "successes." Thus, I'm not signing on to any anthropomorphic deity. I've got a sense of humor, and can appreciate irony as well as the next person, but there's entirely too much suffering and misery not, in any meaningful sense, caused by those bearing the suffering and misery to think it is amusing, or acceptable, or moral to create any Red Herring-God to distract us from our unique role. No compassionate God worth Her/His/Its salt would permit, and in some sense, *cause* this pain. To act in supplication before this insensitive and indifferent, or outright cruel Creature, such craven beings are no more worthy of being considered fully emancipated humans than the twisted "deity" is worthy of being worshipped.

Three

I'm professing belief neither in an anthropomorphic, nor a monotheistic, nor even an extrinsic deity. I'm suggesting that "belief in" an amorphous intrinsic/extrinsic life force that I participate in for the duration I occupy this mortal coil may be as appropriate as the more staid, hide-bound, locked-in-dogma, traditional forms of belief. Scratch that: ...*is more appropriate than...* So, if I'm allowed an *in*trinsic Godhead in a conversation on beliefs, one that is shared, though perhaps not always affirmed, by all Life, then I'm not an atheist—and might actually approximate some Buddhist teachings, without consciously intending to.

I inhabit a life force, or more correctly, the life force inhabits me, for the duration of my life in this expression. *What is death? What happens after life?* Essential questions! What happens to "you" following cessation of corporal functions? While we're at it, let's ask what was happening before "you" came on the scene? You could argue that as far as your consciousness was concerned, pre-life was all void. What makes you think post-life (death) will be any different? What vanity, what arrogance would lead one to think s/he deserved/had coming an eternity of *anything*? (Perchance, as you were when you died? A deaf and blind, toothless, senile 87 year old, seeping body fluids out of all his orifices—Happy Eternity!)

Life has been churning along on this planet for something like 4 ½ billion years; that's a *long* time before you and I, or even *Homo sapiens*, appeared. Despite setbacks little and big, Life is likely to continue churning in all its radiant and vibrant interdependency. Will our species learn moderation, balance, and the repudiation of "Growth" as an operating principle, or will we

179

be an all-too-brief flash in the evolutionary arc of Life? For me, it's an exciting, if not outright anxious, time to be alive, having a vested interest in the continuing survival of my species. In terms of my comprehensive belief system, a lot seems to hang in the near-term balance.

For now, let us remind ourselves how profoundly fortunate we are to have been "born" at all, let alone into this life, in these times, with our unique consciousness, for participation in the Pageant.

Apples/oranges department: observations on perceived dichotomies

1) Heroes vs. victims

I should begin with the caveat that these two terms are not intuitively, intentionally oppositional. *Heroes* suggests *villains* as counterpart while the idea of *victims,* as a result of human agency at least, implies *perpetrators,* or maybe *predators.* However, there is a tendency to equate the casualties/fatalities of our Iraqi debacle—40 to 50 thousand wounded Americans and more than 4200 tragically lost, to say nothing of the Iraqis—to link these perhaps *victims* with heroes, people who have performed heroic deeds. Tragedy it surely is/continues to be; grotesque tragedy, if you want, owing to the preventable nature of our war-on-terror-equals-war-on-Iraq. This still doesn't make our military men and women heroes, in my mind, and I realize I'm on very thin ice here. All sorts of cultural mores and taboos pertain to a nation's brave military fallen. So permit me to attempt a distinction: To the extent a relatively un-self-reflective person allows him/herself to be seduced into imagery of adventure, bravery, glory, honor on behalf of the Fatherland—to say nothing of personal gain—only to discover that s/he has been thrust into a kill-or-be-killed scenario, well, it is very hard for me to see that as heroic. Uncle Sam wants to make a murderer out of you and is willing to make you a casualty in the process.

What is a victim, then? Someone who is hurt or killed through events s/he could not have rationally anticipated. Said events are not precipitated by the victim, thus the sense of randomness arises, particularly in such natural disasters as the Christmas '04 SE Asian tsunami, and more recent Hurricane Katrina in New Orleans. Furthermore, as an example of the limitations we humans place on ourselves, it is not hard to see that the dominant narrative of perhaps all nation-states expects its citizenry to defend the homeland from external threats. Thus, to the extent a citizen answers the presumed need and is duped, or manipulated into accepting the role of defender when no such defense is necessary or justified, I suppose the case can be made that such a person is victimized.

2) Ignorant vs. stupid

It strikes me that there is a tendency to confuse ignorance with stupidity. Surely, we are all ignorant of many things. It is physically not possible to know even significant amounts of everything. The body of knowledge of human experience is simply far too vast for one mind to take it all in (and even if for one moment we could, that knowledge is constantly changing/expanding into new realms). This would be the Eye of God, and we are mere mortals. We should bear the sobriquet *Ignoramus* proudly, but not *too* proudly. We can and sometimes do perceive the interconnectedness that transcends the sub-important false dichotomies (us vs. them) that have plagued us since folks started clotting together in larger groups, say, 10 thousand years ago.

What I don't accept is flaunting one's ethnocentrism; the false pride in "Yeah, I'm a hick cracker suburban/rural American who doesn't bother to stay even superficially informed about this great social experiment we are engaged in, but God made the USA *the* best country in the world!" Such a carefully worded expression of love of God and country literally sends a chill down my back. Conversely, admitting one's ignorance with a willingness to learn—to begin the steps to replace ignorance with knowledge and, dare I say, understanding—is a chance to demonstrate a little humility. Since we all share recognition of our ignorance in various fields of experience, there should be no shame or embarrassment. Not knowing it all is part of the human condition. But it seems to me we are loath to display much in the way of humility—for fear of showing, what, "weakness"?

Stupidity, on the other hand, seems to be a bit trickier to pin down inasmuch as it is often applied as a pejorative *to* people who are not so much lacking in relative knowledge (ignorant) as being apparently unable, or worse, unwilling, to learn. *By* people who presume to "know" something of the particular event in question: *It must be important, if I know it. But you don't know it while having had the opportunity to do so, thus you must be not merely ignorant but stupid.* Begging questions of how one came to possess the dominant interpretation, and issues of substantiation. So, if stupidity is problematic, fraught with affective implications, a kind of ad hominem epithet, does the term have culture-specific validity?

I consider myself stupid if, all things being generally equal, I succumb to the same folly more than twice, and the Spartan among us would make the case that we should learn from one experience; *Life is not a rehearsal*, and all that. I'm stupid for allowing myself to tune out learning opportunities that might benefit me in some unspecified future way, opportunities that traipse across my consciousness like a languid and confident stripper in her slow denouement. I'm mesmerized by the performance but don't compel myself to attend enough for it to qualify as learning, a trade-off between *being/participating* and *standing outside, objectifying, observing*, I suppose. Still, as missing a chance at description, deconstruction, and comprehension of an event, characterizing me as *stupid* is, alas, often a legitimate observation.

3) Anarchy vs. chaos

Simply stated, I take utter chaos to be complete, absolute lack of order/predictability. No pattern discernable; neither rhyme nor reason. The *Abyss*. However, it is possible to imagine less-than-total manifestations of chaos, especially in the realm of human experience. The suspension of social protocols/the normal workings of society, as in the throes or aftermath of a catastrophic occurrence, whether human induced or natural in origin, is a clear example of chaos.

Anarchy, on the other hand, is restricted to human conduct, it seems. It has a decidedly bad reputation these months/years, and I'm not entirely sure why. Anarchy would seem to pertain to the suspension of social conventions, with no established hierarchy of authority in effect, which, of course, could be by design. Thus calling into question the presumption of anarchy as an unalloyed negative. Perhaps deserving of being considered utopian, anarchy on a small social scale—say, a community of 20 people or so?—may be the most enlightened and efficient means of organizing small groups of people. From each according to his/her ability, to each according to his/her need. Larger groups tend to be, at minimum, complicated by the need for representation, which translates into governance perhaps not best served by pure anarchy.

While representative government may be necessary for large communities, cities, states, and regions, arguably that government is best that 1) acts/enacts on behalf of the most constituents, every effort exerted to achieve consensus, and 2) permits, promotes, and encourages the broadest scope of anarchy possible, confined only by the overarching needs of the community. The closer to anarchy, the greater the personal freedom.

4) Freedom vs. license

In terms of interpersonal relationships, license is the use of one's knowledge, power and authority over others for personal pleasure or gain. One acts with license when one manipulates, seduces, or coerces others into doing one's bidding. In terms of the interface between the human and the rest of the biosphere (be that self, family, community, culture, or species), license is acting as if the world's resources were ours to use as we saw fit, as if sustainability and balance and reciprocity were not part of the equation. It is license to be profligate in our use of resources, to presume for one moment that we have *dominion* over all other living things. License is acting as if there were no earthly consequences.

Freedom, on the other hand, is another critter, altogether. On the one hand, the only *pure* freedom a human will come to know is death, *n'est-ces pas?* Everything this side of death, either physiologically or psycho/sociologically, involves a myriad of pushes and pulls, pokes and prods, some of them overwhelming, all of them limitations/constraints on what the mind/body can do. However, given those confines, I propose that freedom in human conduct is limited only by the responsibility to act mindfully and respectfully towards one's fellow humans *and* other biota. Inherent within responsibility is the recognition of the unsustainable nature of humankind's impact on critical niches of the global ecology. Statutory "ownership" does not convey the titleholder the right to profit by pillaging and laying waste the sky, the waterways, or vast tracts of land by the most economically viable means possible. Just as no one is *free* to abuse or enslave his/her fellow human, no one is *free* to pollute or lay waste to the environment. There is no freedom without responsibility.

(2006~'07)

From a letter to an old friend

How goes the struggle? If you have to ask, *What struggle?*, I take it to mean that it is going very well indeed. Either there is no struggle—not consistent with reality—or you've been in the traces so long you're no longer aware of it as a burden. It's "normal," the default position, in the vernacular of the day. You might, of course, ask *Which one?*, since the question is ambiguous as to a particular struggle. In which case, I might have capitalized the "S" so as to imply inclusivity of all of life's vicissitudes. On the other hand, if the statement is nothing more than a formulaic communication-initial utterance (i.e., the sociolinguistic equivalent of *How are ya?* or a grunt, an *Umm, ahhh*; a mechanism to seize the conversational foreground, or signal permission for the speaker to continue), then we can nudge it aside as a frivolous distraction and hope to arrive soon at the main course, the entrée, as it were.

If such a meal exists. Because so far, there is not the slightest hint this letter is even *in the chow line* and time's a'wastin'. Folks have got sheep to mend, fences to shear...

Warning: Linguistics can entice one down some pretty strange rodent burrows. My personal first line of defense is massive amounts of cannabis. When it starts getting really abstruse, I just roll up another torpedo! At what time is it appropriate to cease one's studies? When one is no longer able to roll any more torpedoes, of course...

(January 2004)

Titles

Your humble servant, I remain
        The Elder Left Reverend Tuna Fortuna
Marquis of Mayhem, Prince of Pandemonium
        Bishop of Bent, Squire of Skew
Vicar of Vertigo, Poobah of Poozle (retired)
        Torquemada of Tilt, Wazir of Warp and Woof
Count of Countless Countesses, King of Krazed Krises
        Abbot of Absolution, Emperor of Empathy
Pope of Poop, Duke of Drek
        Captain of Captions, Head of Heads
Saint of Sunder, Potentate of Pot 'n' Toot
        President of Precedents, Chancellor of Chance
Lord of Lewd, Emir of Rhyme
        Admiral of Admirables, General of Generalities
Pilgrim to and from Mirglip, Chief of Chuff

The commons

Our society recognizes two fundamental forms of property. The first, and by far most prevalent in areas where we live, is private ownership. Perhaps as an extension of our Judeo-Christian heritage of *self* as the basic unit of identity/existence, perhaps as an extension of American pioneer-spirit individualism, private property has achieved a kind of apotheosis here: *On this side of the line is my property. I bought and paid for it and, by God, I get to do whatever I want with it. You or somebody else may own the other side of the line; I sacrifice a stake in what happens on your parcel in exchange for absolute sovereignty over mine.* Or some such ethos as this; we all know the drill.

It's the other, lesser valued or taken for granted property that bears more attention. It is the property we all share, the land and landmarks we think so important that no one person or entity should possess it. We believe all have a stake in these legacies. We recognize them as our unique public places, and because they are not ours exclusively, we treat them less reverentially than our private places. But it is precisely because of the contested nature of the commons—with conflicting needs and assumptions getting challenged and played out on a regular basis—that our relationship to the commons bears further consideration.

Assertion: The measure of any social structure is not taken of its citizenry in the private sector, where the power derived from ownership makes decisions about property use essentially unilateral. The appropriate measure of society is in the public arena, the commonweal. How do individuals and groups within the community accommodate conflicting opinions? Does one faction lord it over the others, or do different voices participate in the narrative more or less equitably?

I've been fortunate enough to live near Mt. Tabor Park, one of Portland's few showcase parks, for going on 11 years and I'm not even close to being tired or bored with it. In fact, the better I get to know the park, the more challenging the relationship becomes, and the richer I feel as a result. The *Friends of Mt. Tabor Park* has become the primary vehicle for my giving back to the neighborhood and to the city. Our group comprises a wide range of attitudes and opinions about any conceivable topic. However, I think we all recognize the value of pooling our energies in promoting responsible use, mitigating wear and tear, and waging heroic battles against the invasive botanicals—my own personal vendetta. For various reasons, *We the people* seem to want beautiful public places but don't want to fund them adequately. Our group takes up some of the slack.

The park is an extension of my backyard (almost literally); its welfare is tied to my welfare. It does not bother me in the least that this magnificent hilltop is not mine exclusively. I wouldn't want the exclusive responsibility for its management, and I certainly couldn't afford the taxes. In fact, this is exactly the position I want for myself in relation to Mt Tabor Park: I volunteer time when I can and when I want to help maintain it. I get to choose where I put my energy. Anyone with a stake in its use can participate in ongoing issues, such as off-leash dogs, off-trail mountain bikes, appropriate use of herbicides, security of the reservoirs, and invasive botanicals. I like the feeling that comes in helping to construct a common vision for our neighborhood park's future.

I think you could make the argument that Mt. Tabor Park and the neighborhood serve as a kind of microcosm of the Portland community, to a lesser extent the Pacific Northwest, and lesser still, the country: Mt. Tabor offers us very specific and tangible ways to continue our social experiment of learning how to live together.

(A variation of this essay appeared in *The Southeast Examiner*, January 2006)

Green terrorists

Fellow citizens, beware! Sound the alarm; there are green terrorists about! No, not the folks who want to blow up power lines to save us from ourselves—*but I got your attention, didn't I?*—though in their own way, in our neighborhood, these monsters are just as sinister. I refer, of course, to the vegetative threat lurking in our midst. This moment, in the dead of winter, plants are flinging seeds, settling into new crevices, sending out new fingerling tentacles from which to sprout new life. New plants in new locations where they can quickly overwhelm and displace the native flora. So the *terror* is on a botanical and not a human scale. There is significant "violence" wrought by one species on others but, admittedly, at a much slower pace than we are accustomed to. Since this destruction is not visited upon us directly, the basic question is, why should we care?

I can think of two good reasons to start with; there may be more. The first is aesthetic. If you take walks in our 200-acre neighborhood park, Mt. Tabor, you may catch vistas of a green-monochrome blanket undulating over swatches of the hillside. This is most likely Clematis—though in some areas, it could be Morning Glory—both very aggressive vines that can quickly cover virtually anything in their way. An acre or two that once supported 15 or 20 different indigenous plant species, upon the introduction of, say, Clematis, quickly gets shut down to 5 or 6 holdouts for a more prolonged death by strangulation of nutrients and deprivation of sunlight for photosynthesis. Such a scene is not the way a healthy forest looks. Uniqueness of characteristics that occur interspecies, give way to bland uniformity *intra*species. Thus, Morning Glory blossoms all look very much alike and appear seemingly simultaneously. Whereas of the 20 or so species that the Morning Glory displaced, several would have produced a range of size, coloration, and variation of blossom timing; a far more variegated palette to watch unfold through the seasons.

The other reason to care that our neighborhood and, especially, park are under assault stems from the realization that it is *we* who introduced these aggressors to an otherwise more genteel and dignified contest for the available sunlight, water, and nutrients. The natives, having adapted to the other natives over eons, don't stand a chance. These invaders don't abide by Robert's Rules of Order; they never heard of the Geneva Conventions. They are pillagers, the Plant Kingdom equivalent of 3rd C. Visigoth hordes sacking Rome—*Take no prisoners!* It is no exaggeration that, left unchallenged, the Big Eight invasives could overrun the entire park not already cemented or asphalted. Some, Clematis chief among them, are consolidating vast colonies *despite* occasional, concentrated counter-attacks by valiant Weed Warrior volunteers.

Here, then, are my candidates for the Big Eight Invasive Botanicals of Mt. Tabor Park:

1)   Numero Uno by common infamy, the longest established in the city, county and state and, hence, invader of largest profile is <u>English Ivy</u> (*Hedera helix*).
2)   Arguably, the biggest threat (currently) to Mt. Tabor Park is <u>Clematis</u> (*Clematis vitalba*). Think m.o. of English Ivy but a growth rate five times as fast. And big, fluffy seeds like giant

dandelion seeds, wafting in the breeze. In very few years this vine can completely engulf the canopy of a large Broadleaf Maple, itself having taken 60~80 years to reach such stature, and kill it. Even the mighty Douglas Fir is not immune.

3)   Morning Glory (*Ipomoea ...*) is as good a candidate as any for third place. It spreads quickly and grows fast; it's just not as substantial as Clematis.

4)   I stray from the vine scourges in selecting Scotch Broom (*Cytisus scoparius*). This is an extremely tenacious bush that produces lovely canary-yellow blossoms in late spring (which become thousands of beans/plants by summer), as anyone who has taken a trip outside the city that season can attest. Roadsides, untilled fields, clear cuts, virtually every open space west of the Cascades gives way to this nasty opportunist.

5)   Slightly less a menace locally than Scotch Broom is Climbing, or Deadly Nightshade (*Solanum dulcamara*), another vine. Delicate purple blossoms in summer produce bright red berries that birds love to eat—probably gets 'em stoned—the seeds of which are then deposited everywhere. Which is where this plant grows.

6)   A low-growing bush (3~5 ft.), Tansy Ragwort (*Senecio jacobaea*) is potentially a more serious threat than it currently is. Like Scotch Broom, at the first indication of this plant's blooming cycle, when the plant is recognizable at 100 feet, neighborhood Weed Warriors have been somewhat successful at pulling up all we encountered, thus holding the line against their incursions over the last few years.

7)   This addition to the list is a bit of an anomaly in our park and neighborhood: In Mt Tabor Park there is only one known patch of Japanese Knotweed (*Polygonum cuspidatum*) and it has been under siege, contained but unresigned, for seven years. A fiendish cousin of bamboo(?), this plant loves damp slopes, sends

runners in all directions very quickly, and can grow 8~10 feet tall. And unlike many other invasives, this one is impossible to pull up; digging it up is slow and painstaking. It has become, in a very short time, the #1 invasive in many valley and coastal riparian areas; it is *so* aggressive that despite a respite we may currently enjoy from this plant locally, we shouldn't relax our vigil. Based on the plight of other wetlands in our region from the onslaught of Knotweed, it will be back.

8)   Himalayan Blackberry (*Rubus discolor*) rounds out the list. It does grow quickly sending out canes that loop over branches, even young trees; when the cane touches ground it roots again establishing a new plant base. Unquestionably, the blackberry displaces native species that have no defense against it. There is a feature, however, that in a small way, redeems/mitigates this plant's existence: it produces a delicious berry in late summer that is worth the risk of thorns slashing at one's forearms and hands. Ranked in a list of difficult to uproot/eradicate, the blackberry is *not* near the top.

All this, of course, begs the question, Why a list of exactly eight invasive botanicals? Why not fewer; why not more? Simply put, these eight represent the most conspicuous invasives in our park *at this time*. These are the mega-flora intent (if that's not too strong a term) on crowding out every species in their way. While you sleep, *they* are becoming further entrenched, better established, growing.

This list should be reviewed frequently, maybe twice a year, for updates; the status of these and many other species are very much in play. Finally, a *Dishonorable* Mention, a menace that is not (yet?) a problem on Mt. Tabor is Giant Hogweed (*Heracleum mantegazzianum*), a noxious, spiny weed poisonous

196

to the touch. A "recent" arrival from the Steppes of Russia, it is an environmental terrorist, if ever there was one.

If you'd like to help win back to relative ecological stability our treasure of a neighborhood park, the Weed Warriors, a branch of Friends of Mt. Tabor Park (FMTP), in conjunction with local parks personnel, sponsor several work projects with counterattacks on the invasive species always a focus. These events occur on the last Saturday of the month throughout the spring/summer/fall. For details, contact FMTP…

(An edited version of this article was published in the Portland *Southeast Examiner*, February 2006)

Departures without arrival
(No place to go)

Searchin' high and low, tryin' to figure who to be.
No place to go same as anyplace will do.
Stumblin' into paradise; what is it that I see?
No place to go same as anyplace will do.
Sittin' in some shameless shambles,
       feelin' kinda blue.

Checkin' out the agitation, scheming who to sue.
All set up to run this race, they gimme just one shoe.
A complicated plot this has and we ain't got a clue.

We got no place to go same as anyplace will do.
No place to go same as anyplace will do.
But anyplace is everyplace and this will have to do.

No place to go same as anyplace will do.
No place to go same as anyplace will do.
Oo-o wee, lemme outa here!
No place to go… same as anyplace will do.

(The nexus of a blues/rock song, Fall 2005)

On giving

Many years ago my grandparents, as a consequence of having much free time on their hands, took up number painting. Since they enjoyed this experience, there was nothing for it but to insure their grandsons got some hands-on *art* in the Christmas stocking. These "paintings" came as a kit with the paints, brushes, and a jigsaw patterned and numbered canvass, complete instructions included. Making anyone who could count and not color-blind a veritable Gainsborough. I know because I kept for years, as a testament of my grandparents' love, my own personal *Blue Boy* tucked carefully away in a closet somewhere.

My problem ran thus: While I loved my grandparents very much (and thereby loved their act of love in the giving), I didn't at all "love" these paintings. It isn't logically incumbent on the recipient to love the object—the gift—in order to love my grandparents; one is not a necessary consequence of the other. It was unfortunate, however, that their love for me, while genuine enough, was so unrealistic in its appraisal of my tastes and needs. So many miles apart; such a changed world, their lives to mine!

Segue some sixty years later: Ain't it funny how the ol' Cosmic Wheel spins? I have seven grandchildren. It's my chance to experience the situation from a grandparent's perspective: What "Blue Boys" am I apt to inflict on them?

Part Four

Grackle's thorn: Hercules Aphid

Grackle's longest-running connection, short his relationship to Maggie, his younger sister by three years, was Hercules Mountain Aphid, variously over the decades a bosom buddy, distant acquaintance, object of cautious curiosity, and just another irascible malcontent, who, depending on his demeanor on the occasion in question, was to be treated warily. Herk and Grackle went back to state university days—dorm roommates part of that time—half a century previously. Sophomore year was spent in dissolute camaraderie, in Larry's Lower Level, the university student union, where they shot pool or played the card game Hearts with other feckless students for hours at a time. Occasionally, they'd make the one-hour run to the nearby Mexican border city for an evening in the fleshpots of Canal Street, sowing oats and courting STDs—one toss, six bucks American. And here they were, after all this time, residing in the same city, their houses mere blocks away on parallel streets.

Despite this extensive, and often intensive, history together, in many significant aspects of personality it would be difficult to conjure a more contrasting set of individuals. Over the decades some of those points of contrast became more entrenched, a simmering stew of complaints, less apt to be ignored or accommodated as they accumulated and bubbled over; a dreary duality, indeed. Though it wasn't obvious at first, the annoyances had come to loom larger than the years of shared discovery. The niggling thorns sum totally had come to be not worth enduring. They had entered into a phase of mutually agreed upon estrangement. Grackle for the most part was relieved it had happened.

Few people would characterize Grackle as shy or reticent or withholding of his thoughts on any given topic, once engaged in polite discourse. By contrast, however, Hercules often exhibited a runaway ego. To call him a motor mouth would be unkind to machines, which with minimal maintenance operate as designed for decades. When no longer needed, a simple flip of the switch shuts down the entire apparatus. Give ol' Herk access to an audience, however, and he could crank out the shuck and jive for hours—long past the desire by anyone else to participate any longer in the event. No cutoff switch. Grackle knew this all too well; he'd watched examples of "the performance" beyond counting—one of perhaps 25 or 30 routines, each delivered in a different time and place, and hopefully to a different audience, but the same performer, and essentially a variation of the same performance. Herkimer would rather work a room than eat, and the boy *did* like his chow time. His garrulousness was matched by the zeal with which he would attack the food portion in front of him, and he had the corpulent physique to show for it. Who knows? Maybe he thought his serving would be taken from him if he didn't hoover it—on the high setting—though he had no family history of such poverty, or food deprivation.

Before an audience he was indefatigable. He spent so much time talking/preparing his next response that he rendered himself unable to hear anything but the crudest outline of the offering of others, those timorous few who might venture a brief comment when a scant pause presented itself.

As such things often go, Herk had been reinforced (by Momma, certainly) in early childhood for some cute little routine, invariably comedic, that he'd come up with to set himself apart from a two-year-older brother. With Mom's encouragement over the weeks and months Herk polished the timing, but more specifically the form, of the delivery. Soon he learned he could pick topics almost at random and apply his own cornpone take, to the delight and amusement of one and all. The first time. Actually, even the second time, because the observer could note Herk's stylistic preferences. This awareness came to Grackle rather slowly, long after the second hearing. But soon enough, with repeated tellings, he'd come to recognize the routine early into the narrative. Ol' Herk didn't memorize the shtick word for word. The performance varied by a word here, a rephrased comment there, and it still wound up with his first-time audience not knowing the difference but enjoying the anecdote. Over the years he burnished his persona and cultivated mechanisms and techniques to draw in the discursive commentary, the connection of an uttered word or phrase to remind him of a similar experience. To be sure, he was a polished performer; *All the world's a stage* and Herk was always on.

The man was a born-salesman. What's he selling? you ask. He's selling Hercules Mountain Aphid, of course. He was the first of his family to receive a Bachelor's Degree, let alone a Master's. Straight out of high school, Herk, pursued the eminently practical degree of Master of Business Administration. *Practical* was the watchword for Herk; he had no time or patience for useless coursework of literature back in college days. He was heard to boast of not reading fiction—*a waste of time.* No frivolous studies of history, graphic arts, poetry, mythology, comparative religions, or (*gasp!*) philosophy—the sort of studies that are generally considered the basis of a well-rounded education, an expanded perspective of the world for informed citizenship, and a basic knowledge of the civilization from which we've sprung. Even the social sciences (e.g., sociology, anthropology, psychology) got short shrift, were deemed superfluous to the main purpose and function of an ambitious late-20th century man, which was a keen understanding of the marketplace in order to tap into and siphon off an income stream from somewhere amidst the supply-and-demand machinations.

You might assume that because Herk had decided to focus his academic attention on market principles at the cost of the arts and humanities, he might exhibit the slightest humility or modesty in venturing observations of social events. In that assumption, you would be mistaken. Without any hesitation Mr. Aphid was ready to seize the conversational forefront; had, in fact, been looking for his opening since the interaction commenced.

Needless to say, having Herk represent a product or service for a variety of businesses was very successful strategy for many years through several employment iterations, the common thread being his *born to sell* attitude. If it's all an act, then clearly a premium is accorded the adaptable person, the one who best adapts to new situations, as the best icebreaker, preferably through the use of humor. The man definitely had the knack.

However, from Herk's third telling of the same witty vignette, and thereafter, the listener was apt to cast about for an escape—lest some spontaneous form of mayhem transpire. The variations of the telling were purely stylistic, not critical to the mechanics; one really didn't need to hear the amusing anecdote again. Ever. Nonetheless, over the years Grackle had occasionally fallen prey to attending socially obligatory events with Herk, winding up stuck, and thereby being a captive audience—too many times. Grackle could recognize a routine, among the several dozen of his repertoire, sometimes from the first sentence or two, a routine that might take three or four minutes to set up properly and bring off with a flourish.

By about now the reader is beginning to wonder, why would this grumpy, introverted misanthrope hang out with Mr. Social Gadfly if the outcome was so predictable and onerous? The answer is not so straightforward or simple. A relationship, even a strained relationship patched together over decades, is bound to have threads of vague but familiar interdependence, even co-dependence. Not to mention, a familiar antidote for loneliness. Some of one's shared connections can be instrumental as to how one thinks/reacts to aspects of society. Even a casual survey would indicate that many relationships continue via inertia. There were compelling reasons to set the connection in motion initially, and without resistance the connection continued expanding out from itself, like a spiraling nautilus, a Fibonacci Sequence.

Grackle, for all his failings, cultivated the intent of attending to issues of social inequality, not to mention environmental degradation. Though it was a source of some anxiety, he promoted and projected a stance of outward involvement and concern, some of which approached the realm of the philosophical, perhaps even spiritual. By contrast, Herk's overweening self-aggrandizement established him firmly in the flock of a *geistliche tiefflieger*—a spiritual low-flyer.

The thing that was so annoying for Grackle about interactions with a persona locked into serial routines was that most of the time the opportunity for genuine here-and-now interactions got short-circuited and sacrificed. Meanwhile, with each additional anecdotal retelling, the entertainment value slipped a notch…. However, here's an interesting point: Despite occasional psychic meltdowns when events were not going the way he thought they should, Herk manifested indications that he was by-and-large content with his lot. He did not act as if he bore any particular burden beyond the random, day-to-day litany of things that go wrong for everybody: a malfunctioning garage door, acid indigestion/constipation, a suspicious noise from the engine of his vehicle at normal operating speeds, a termagant spouse. He managed to cope with these vicissitudes as well as anyone, better than many, without too much fanfare. However, as to big-picture, worldview, motivating principle(s), there didn't seem to be anything substantive, nothing apparently driving Hercules beyond his own personal aspirations.

Aspects of the Grackle Pisswing/Hercules Aphid approach/ avoidance over such a long and complicated time frame can only be considered *organically*, as they say. In any case, the depth and complexity of that shared history was a prominent reason why the relationship had continued as long as it did.

Grackle's superficial exploration of the Rabbit psychometric survey for evidence of his own mental well-being turned up a secondary and unanticipated finding. He was able to associate a number of attributes clustered within Factor One with his long-time associate, Hercules Aphid. The psychopathy variant this referred to was called "Aggressive Narcissism." Ol' Herk would certainly score high in traits such as "glibness/superficial charm, grandiose sense of self-worth," at least some degree of "cunning/manipulative, shallow affect, with genuine emotion

208

short-lived and egocentric," and "callousness, with a lack of empathy." This Narcissistic Personality Disorder (NPD) shared a correlation with low anxiety, low empathy, but high scores on achievement scales, and "social potency," Also, this group scores as a low suicide risk. (Such folks just love themselves too much, it seems.) It was as if these descriptors were written with Herk in mind. There were as many as a quarter of the traits that didn't seem to fit Herk's persona, but in general most seemed uncannily apt. You may be sure this discovery gave Grackle a lot to chew on.

Grackle understood, as a bona fide septuagenarian, that he was bound to harbor an unsavory trait (treat?) or three himself, internalized and all but unrecognizable to him, but thoroughly apparent, even blatant to those in his close circle. Who didn't? Especially in this country, where arguably Individualism, the celebration of self, reaches its apotheosis. Nonetheless Graculous imagined himself to show restraint, even reticence as a matter of course in order to better comprehend the nuanced presentation of his interlocutors. True, he could be goaded into reacting heatedly, even forcefully, but such incidences were not common. He needed socialization like most other humans, but in brief doses preferably in the company of small groups. Interspersed with periods of quiet introspection. Large group interactions for long periods of time were exhausting, and therefore to be avoided or minimized whenever possible. It was just the opposite for Herk, who craved the rapt, upturned faces in wondrous amazement. As an inveterate blowhard, he never met a conversation he couldn't dominate, or turn to his advantage. Herk was the hebephrenic to Grackle's catatonia.

Grackle and Herk, both, grew up under the auspices of a Protestant framework, which was eminently useful in terms of social contacts in that community. Having newly entered that hormonally challenged stage of life, access to the young ladies—even socially proscribed access—was worth any trial. Hoops of fire or Presbyterian rituals and protocol, it was paying to play.

Parenthetically, it had occurred to Grackle more than once that the entire concept of civilization itself, at least at the level of "polite society," rests upon the tacit agreement by men on behalf of women, the stewards and custodians of culture, to toe the line, show manners, submit to social standards, and behave in a civil manner —all in order not to have to struggle continuously for sex.

In any event, Christianity did not seem to stick as a theological or moral beacon for either. Without the overt Christian program as guide, what took its place? Somehow Herk was able to remain unfazed and unburdened by the environmental/geopolitical/ economic or social crises looming on the horizon. Willingly oblivious, in step with a large majority of Americans.

Inertia would seem to impel *more of the same*. The momentum of decades, if not centuries, augurs for little or no socially initiated change. Especially since the change would require in almost every way a shrinkage: *Don't ask me to give up the lifestyle I earned. It's what my parents and grandparents fought to achieve in their day. Try to shut off the petroleum spigot, or access to God-given resources in any way, and you'll have a blood revolution on your hands!*

Still, how does society in general, Herk in particular, manufacture disbelief?

[M]ost men...are in a strange uncertainty about [life], whether it is of the devil or of God, and have somewhat hastily concluded that it is the chief end of man here to "glorify God and enjoy him forever."

Henry David Thoreau, "Walden"

In Grackle's case, he was left with somesort of vague animist/secular-humanist orientation, which was terrific for fostering a richer, deeper identity with Nature. However, it offered precious little to sustain witness and seek redress to the wholesale profligacy and plunder of Earth's resources— effectively wherever humans encountered them. The forests, the fisheries, the soil, the very air we breathe and water we drink: most were imperiled in most quarters, and becoming more so. As such a social outcast, this view made it a struggle for him to cultivate normal everyday pleasantries and platitudes, let alone generate a passingly credible conviviality and enthusiasm among his acquaintances. Thus, in and out of relationship with Hercules and others, the profound mystery of what made Grackle tick, the scope and intricate evocation of his cadenza, was an ongoing puzzle; the How and Why of the man, the enduring conundrum.

Opacity

You want certitude?
Wanting of itself
isn't apt to change much.
How about perfection?
It's probable that people aspire
to more, beyond, over the rainbow
even though so much is unknowable
unobtainable for us
fickle, finite, fallible creatures.
If it's clarity and straightforward
predictability you are after
you search the wrong field.
Try mathematics. Or syllogisms.
You'd better leave language alone.
Language is an inexact means
of interpreting our place
in the universe, never mind
verbal communication is
the best we've got.
Some would say
the whole ball game.

Too much/not enough

For a long time I used to think that, as my own personal curse, I was a little too world-wary to be easily gulled by the standard brand hucksters, just savvy enough not to fall prey to the garden-variety chum proffered for my hard-earned money—but not nearly smart, wise, or worldly enough to come to terms/make peace with our collective failure to address our greatest problems. Failure to actually promote concordance that we face such issues as overpopulation, in relation to widespread evidence of imperiled or collapsing ecologic niches on which magnitudes of biologic interconnectedness depend. Issues such as climate change…highest levels of CO_2 in the atmosphere (390+ ppm) in at least the last 2.1 *Million* years. Our failure to transition from fossil fuels to carbon-neutral energy sources is stunning in its myopic self-indulgence (but that's just how the free-market economy works!). This generation will bear the "distinction" of bringing down the House, our *Eikos,* despite culpability extending back two generations, at least; said culpability extending to the generations that knew there were going to be serious consequences to their resource exploition rapine—and plundered full steam ahead, anyway.

Thus, it is not difficult for the reader to detect my disquietude—a clear reflection of my inability to shrug it off as *not my problem,* and inability to imagine strategies to get my fellow hominids off their collective arses and make substantive changes for the good of themselves as well as future generations. In conspicuous discomfort, I seem to be stuck in between. A

213

condition not unlike what Siddhartha faced as he entered his journey of discovery. It is said, we all possess elements of the Buddhahood.

Like I said, I *used* to inhabit this unsettled and uncomfortable limbo of "can't help but notice" on the one hand and "no meaningful, productive moderation or mitigation pending" on the other. Lately, however, I've noticed a diminishing anxiety regarding my sense of guilt for our collective sins; I seem to wax more docile, and not as fired up by the litany of unsustainable "crimes of our times" as I used to be. Furthermore, I have a growing suspicion this correlates with the piecemeal, chipping-away deterioration of my brain functions.

For me, arguably, this is a good thing, bringing the horizons in closer. I certainly don't have the stamina of the *young turks* of today, for the cornucopia of intellectual challenges, and I doubt I have the quickness or acuity. Still, I maintain old age itself need not be a curse (to me, anyway). Or perhaps it is a less-onerous curse than being suspended between the horns or our collective, game-changing failures, and dubious "successes."

Intent on finding

Intent on finding strength
he carefully examined himself
in the looking glass
and, approving the visage,
moved on to more important tasks.

His brother, searching
for weakness, could not fail
to find it; suspicion confirmed
he cast aside the glass rudely
which in breaking amplified
his weakness many fold.

(Prescott, AZ 1963)

Voluntary solitary

You know, I once coveted an utterly solitary life, that is to say absolute isolation from all ongoing human contact. Had I the means at the time, I'm certain I would have attempted it. Over the years I had taken the substance of human interaction as so venal, self-serving, and hugely demanding—while so little rewarding—that I was prepared to turn my back on it altogether, and create an environment to suit a simple rustic's basic needs in complete exile. It was all very Thoreau-esque, to be sure.

Too much was I a product of my age and nationality. Years of exposure to this society, its seductions and false promises, led me to question the value of continuing my participation in the social structure. Recognizing my plight fed the flames of my frustration. I would not have my life and the sum of its energies contorted, or rendered impotent by the mainstream social construction, a definition that fosters 1) greed, which flourishes from not trusting that there is enough to share, and 2) fear, which comes from the feeling of vulnerability and inadequacy, as a result of the false divisions that nonetheless separate us.

Was I channeling the ghost of ol' Henry David? In any event, I would not succumb to the Siren, if I could help it. Thus, I conceived of building this sanctuary in the wilderness… Who could say? If I took along the right tools to explore and satisfactorily define myself over time, maybe I would be prepared to return to the Family, bearing or being borne on the shield of principled self-discovery. Resigned to the discord and strife that seems to characterize humanity, late 20th/early 21st century. Resigned, or somehow seeing through and beyond it....

This reclusive vision occurred a long time ago—around my mid-20s, I imagine; after at least my first trip to Europe and two years later, through Mexico, Central America, and back again, but before I'd developed much of a circle of friends, especially of the feminine persuasion. I likewise imagine any psychotherapist worth his/her salt would recognize in this a juvenile petulance, not yet having my social worth recognized and fully validated by all. Pouty reaction: pick up my marbles and go home.

Much later, as fate would have it, I had an extended opportunity to live with all the solitude I could stand, thank you. I bought rural property and for a while lived there with my family, my brother's family nearby. After some years, that idyll abruptly changed and I was left there alone, with both families having moved on to greener pastures. It was some of the most heart-wrenchingly lonely months of my life; quite enough time on my hands to examine my flawed and apparently pointless existence until I was thoroughly sick of myself. And contrary to my more youthful and naïve expectations, the Great Outdoors wasn't helping.

It dawned on me but slowly that the solitude, with no one else to bounce ideas, characterizations, and interpretations off of, was more conducive to psychopathy than self-awareness or growth under those conditions. One does not get to define him/herself outside of a human context. *No man is an island.* No one is an entirely "self-made" man. It is only through interaction with other people—or so I have concluded—a range of interpersonal connections with many other people, that we become socialized, that we are made human. And not off on some Robinson Crusoe adventure getting in touch with one's primitive nature.

I now believe that for optimal mental health, I need neither isolation from nor total immersion in humanity for long periods. Just as too much isolation can turn you in on yourself to no good end, too much exposure to human interaction could dissolve your agile, fluid, creative essence into something automaton-like and expedient. Finding that shifting balance point between these potential extremes becomes all-important.

In my case, I fully recognize that too much socialization, as well as too much isolation, are not good for my equanimity. So I am, with practice, more or less able to cycle from one episode to its counterpart, staying near that kind of median line. Most of my time is spent in the urban, socially dictated environment. I perform adequately, I suppose, but it makes me appreciative of my every-other-month chance to escape to my Small River sanctuary.

There, after a few days without hot, running water or electricity, light via kerosene lamps and candles, heat thanks to firewood from a wood stove, I am unabashedly delighted to return to comforts and conveniences of my city home—minus the rodents! So goes the cycle.

Civic accountability: an application for employment

"Have you ever been convicted of a crime?"

Yes, twice:

1) On March 20, 2006, 19 people, including myself, engaged in non-violent civil disobedience in our senior senator's Portland office. Our goal was to confer with Senator Wyden or, failing that, his chief of staff, regarding our desire to have the senator initiate legislation to begin removing American military personnel from Iraq. Some six hours later Federal Marshals arrested, processed, and released us on the misdemeanor charge of failure to obey a command by a federal officer (failure to vacate the premises as ordered). Through negotiations with federal prosecutorial staff, I pleaded guilty to the charge and as a result, completed the 10 hours' community service "punishment" in Mt. Tabor Park, where I frequently volunteer work anyway.

2) In early spring of 1968, in Tucson, AZ, I was tried on three misdemeanor counts (unlawful assembly, disturbing the peace, and—I've forgotten—blocking a right of way?). Along with 16 others, I had attempted to impede a bus full of military conscripts on their way to basic training, and then on to Vietnam, where they would quickly be thrust in a situation of *kill or be killed.* I was found guilty on two of the three counts and placed on probation for three years. Questions of the legitimacy of

219

America's military presence in Vietnam were not allowed in the trial.

We all grew up

We all grew up with
everybody knows
grow, hoe, show yer votes
flow, tow, blow the boats
stow, throw, sow yer oats gently
through the seam merrily
et cetera life is
but a(n improbable) *dream*
you remember how it goes?
a notion to row downstream
no reason a decision an excuse
to row an inconceivable upstream
is simply not feasible… so what?
Ly fis butad ream: since when
did that matter? Everybody's nose
warily, verily, airily, scarily
wife to go
            with cream.

A good burn: the scream of salmonberry

Few things satisfy like a good burn. I'm talking about a well-laid bonfire with lots of combustible material piled into a mound, maybe 5 to 6 feet high. If that really catches—reaches critical incendiary mass—well, that's when the heart quickens. Feel the heat on your face and, through your clothes, the rest of your body. Hear the roar and crackle as the waste wood and cut brush begin to be consumed. Watch the flames leap 20 to 30 feet into the sky, the sparks and still-burning fragments still higher. The smell, too, can be pleasant; a whiff of the fire in the shifting breeze is part of the experience.

A successful fire takes some engineering; the wetter the fuel, the more carefully the core needs to be planned. Even a fire of very wet material is, of course, possible; the last time I got a burn going it had rained off and on the previous night and into that morning. Fortunately, I'd brought a lot of dry newspaper and cardboard. A good foundation of burning cardboard will support igniting evergreen branch tips. Dried or green, the resin in the tips and needles catch very quickly and burn very hot. After that, start piling on the tops of salmonberry cuttings/up-rootings, again, whether green, wet, or well-dried is an insignificant variable at this point. As this lot begins to catch, throwing on bigger and heavier branches or trunks of the local species (alder, maple, cascara, vine maple, cedar, fir, hemlock, cherry, native filbert, elderberry, etc.) would be a good idea.

By this time, with a little assistance from Prometheus or one of those fire deities, you've charged a raging core so hot that it combusts practically everything you can throw at it at an incredible rate. And your heart is pounding out of your chest. If you're not too impervious, a good fire can seduce you onto psychic journeys to exotic locations of awareness you wouldn't have known existed. I've known big fires and their aftermaths that were decidedly hypnotic in their power to draw you into them.

It is not difficult for me to conjure a kind of *archetypal* blaze, friend of man (thanks to Prometheus): Source of warmth and light. Means for cooking raw materials into more palatable/ digestible food. Weapon with which to ward off creatures that would prey on us. Suspend the verbal narrative and a decent blaze is apt to have a trance-inducing effect.

Longer-dead but damp material will sometimes sputter and crackle as it is slowly consumed but it's the green, fresh-cut vegetation that generates most of the shrieks. A clinical study would probably yield something to the effect that moisture and/or sap trapped in channels inside a thicker, more rigid sheath build up pressure as the moisture-converted-to-steam expands from the heat. As the gas escapes through the woody covering, the host plant can release an eerie, whistle-like scream. Though we draw reasonable assumptions about the probable physiological explanation of this phenomenon, the death throes of the burning vine maple or salmonberry can cause them to perform in a way that you are not apt to experience in any other context. Expiring, as they give up the ghost to tongues of flame, they sing a shrill farewell. And the contrast between the human scream and a fresh-cut salmonberry stalk is noteworthy. Under extreme duress, a human might muster a 15 to 20 second shriek before having completely exhaled, whereas it's not uncommon for a salmonberry to wail its perfidious demise 30 seconds uninterrupted. It's enough to give you pause. Is this the spirit in the plant life surrendering to another form? Is this an expression of *Animism*?

Fire is a useful tool; with care and patience, it is among the best. At one point, in my "homesteading" career, I thought to compost brush cuttings by sending stalks, leaves, etc., through a chipper I'd bought secondhand. Not only was it a slow, noisy process using petroleum, the chipper didn't beat the pieces small enough to break down at all quickly. And some of those chunks would end up sprouting into new plants. Well, then I'd just stack the cut brush into big piles and wait for them to compost on their own, which they would do years after they served as scaffolding/ protection for the next generation of blackberry or salmonberry. So really, torching the puppies is the most direct, expedient means.

Talk about utility, short of a D6~D8 Cat to root around the base of an old fir stump and then finally push/pull it out, fire is far and away the best, and may be the only way to "get rid" of it. A mature tree was taken off the stump back in the 1950s in what is now near the entrance to my meadow. Said stump stood about 5 feet off the surrounding terrain. By the 70s and 80s, it supported a thriving colony of blue and red huckleberries, salal and native trailing blackberries, among others. On a tear recently to beat back more of the brush in the meadow surrounding my cabin, I started brush fires against one side of the vegetative mass surrounding the stump and after a year and a half of perhaps seven or eight burns, the stump has been consumed down to the surrounding grade and even below it in places.

To be sure, the burn has left a conspicuous scar, maybe 30 feet in diameter. But vegetation will be growing on this scar within two years. After all, the Coast Range of Oregon is a temperate rainforest: not as hot as the Willamette Valley in the summer, but not as cold in winter, owing in no small part to the proximity of the largest body of water in the world. The Pacific Ocean almost always directly determines the weather on the coast and in the Coast Range: wet most or all of spring; wet some or all of fall; continuously wet all winter. Moderate temperatures. Usually dry and warm, rarely hot (50s~90s F.) in summer, this area exhibits all the characteristics of temperate rainforest. Plants compete in a wild scramble for access to the available sun and water, springing from moderately rich soil, and many species do very well. If I am to maintain the meadow at its current perimeter, and perhaps a little larger, I must be eternally vigilant against the resurgence of several botanicals, Salmonberry primarily, but Blackberry is getting well established—thus, a never-ending supply of bonfire material.

I readily admit this is a Sisyphusian task and one sure to occupy me for the rest of my life. Fact is, I'm resigned to Salmonberry and/or blackberry sprouting from my grave within six months of my demise. In the meantime, I have plenty of reason to say, *Better living through "applied" pyromania!*

(Winter 2005/06)

225

Cosmic justice

Circumstances sometimes jostle me from my unconscious mode of operation (the *default position*) such that I cannot help but attend to and acknowledge the crazy course of events that comprises my life, and ponder how it came to be so. Two separate events relating to my *physical* condition inspired this conjecture; the perils of my *mental* well-being are allegedly more frequent and familiar, and are, in any case, taken up in other texts.

I

Early in 2004, on one of those rare occasions when one is suddenly taken by the inexplicable urge to physical self-improvement, I launched into a series of simple, mostly isomorphic exercises. Over the last couple decades I'd more or less settled on a handful of basic exercises I could perform on the floor, usually in scant, comfortable attire. I'll mention a few: Lying flat on my back I do some arches, leg lifts, lower back strengtheners in general. Then I turn over and do a set of pushups from the knees (*not* the toes). And while it would be a good idea *every*time, I only sometimes start the whole regimen with a stand up round of wrist, arm, and shoulder exercises with a pair of 10 lb. dumbbells.

On the day in question I'd foregone the dumbbells and so when I commenced my *wuss* pushups, I did so without the benefit of relevant muscle-group warm ups, a now-universally accepted prerequisite to any serious workout. (But not when I was growing up. Nobody talked about honest-to-god warm-ups; you just plunged into whatever activity you were called upon to perform.) I'm used to running off 12 to 15 of these pushups—there really is a lot less weight to raise with the knees as pivot instead of the toes. In this instance, in the 2nd or 3rd push I felt (*heard?*) this slowed pop in my left shoulder and, with only a little burning sensation but no real pain, I continued on. After completing a set, I usually take a short break before coming back to another dozen or so reps, but on this occasion, by the end of the break the vague burning sensation could be more specifically identified as unambiguous *pain*—further pushups were definitely ill-advised.

In 63 years I have of course damaged this or that portion of my anatomy but nary a broken bone (with the exception mentioned below, *Oh, arboreal Druids, hear my knock!*) and damage to musculature heretofore had always resulted in effective recovery over time, so I was reasonably optimistic at my prospects as I massaged my shoulder…

II

I'm not prone to illness, having gone 3~4 years in recent memory without so much as a cold. However, in early October 2004, I had contracted and succumbed to a full chest infection (*The wages of sin?* Who knows…) that made it almost impossible to breathe for the first few days before settling into a low grade fever, weakness/fatigue, and a wracking cough as I tried to clear enough lung to catch my breath through the buckets of mucus I was producing. I rested, drank lots of fluids, took very hot baths, slept 16~18 hours a day, and consumed massive amounts of vitamin C in addition to a full complement of other vitamins and minerals. Furthermore, I was completely ascetic regarding my usual vices—wine, chocolate, coffee, and ganja—for over two weeks. Slowly, painfully slowly, I dragged myself back from what seemed in those first few daze the brink of death.

By coincidence, I'd contrived one of my bachelors' gatherings to take place later in the month at my Oregon coast-range hovel. During these outings, these periodic escapes from domesticity and the city routine, I am joined by a small confederacy of male peers. Logistics make it difficult to get away very often so I plan these events carefully and sometimes more than a month in advance. In this case, by the beginning of October the available slot had been established as a three-day window immediately before Halloween—before I became sick. But my Herculean efforts at recovery had paid off; by the time of the scheduled outing, I'd nursed myself back maybe 75~80% to normal strength and stamina, in no little part by being abstemious.

But when the *boyos* fetch up creek they are apt to treat the event more in terms of a toot than anything resembling asceticism. Escape from civilization implies dispensing with generally-held conventions, such as bathing and serious grooming/cleanliness. Linguistic niceties are summarily dispensed with. Sounds that result from the process of metabolizing ingested materials punctuate the conversation. The quality and timing of comestibles are generally held to be secondary to the quality of intoxicants, *timing* being essentially continuous. You get the idea. The word *binge* has purchase; the phrase, *Any excuse for a party!* resonates rather uniformly. Overall, there's a sense of subdued revelry—you've got to pace yourself when you get to be our age.

In addition to the single-minded pursuit of the art of functional inebriation, we usually attend to various projects around the manse; of course an impaired state only adds to the challenge. A brush fire largely from salmonberry hacked from the periphery of the meadow is always on the list, weather permitting. Driveway maintenance and firewood acquisition also feature prominently. After three daze of sustained self-abuse and sporadic labor, we are more than a little happy to return to our wives and domesticity (yes, I admit it), ready to shoulder the traces for another 2~3 months until the next bacchanalia can be contrived.

On that particular day, it was raining pretty hard when I got up creek, off loaded the essentials, and checked out the place. Since I was wet and the place was damp, a fire was the first order of the day. Plugging in the water system should have been the second, but the rain never let up and the warmer and dryer I got, the more I just wanted to melt into the sofa until one of my co-conspirators arrived (note: no house water; dehydration already an issue). Sure enough, Tumor and Grunt arrived a short while later and the reconvening commencement exercise entailed slashes of Yukon Jack, a round of beer, and a pipe and/or spliff in no particular order. The astute reader can already conjure the next chapter of this woebegone tale. I'll merely provide a few of the salient details.

Not long into this conviviality, I began to notice that all was not well; my day was approaching an abyss. To head that off I got up from the table and navigated my way to the kitchen where I found some water (that someone must have brought in) and had a drink. I stood for a moment adjusting to the standing position, one hand on the counter, the other holding a cup of water, I believe, starting a response to a comment Grunt or

Tumor, seated at the table, had uttered immediately before. Then, lights out. I'd relaxed my vigilance and my demons saw their chance: Sucker-punched! One minute I'm standing there feeling pretty sick—but not sicker than I'd been 5 or 10 minutes before, or easily 5 or 10 times before —and the next minute I'm in a crumpled bloody pile on the floor. That'd never happened to me before.

There's not a twinge of boast in admitting I've been horrifically sick to my stomach before and I've passed out on more than one occasion owing to my own folly. Hey, what can I say? For every new experience, discovery of the *golden mean* is a new process; *moderation* gets renegotiated. They've been hard lessons…

In the few prior instances, I'd had some notion that unconsciousness was approaching and could catch myself, break the fall, protect my face with my arms/hands. This time I was completely gone in a full upright position. It must have looked like an old building that, with the deft positioning of explosives, implodes with a lot of noise and dust but no damage to surrounding real estate. Except that, in this case, the adjacent 'real estate' counted coup on me. I must have smacked the counter surface head cocked slightly to the right; I hit the left corner of my wire-rimmed glasses frame, smashing it into my face, breaking my nose. Then, I seemed to have raked the top of my head across the edge of the counter top before catching at least the top three drawer knobs in my descent, chaffing a swatch off my scalp.

I can't have been gone more than 2~3 seconds. I don't remember the calamitous descent at all, but I remember hearing the scrape of chairs on floor as Tumor and Grunt leapt up at the resounding collision of me and the floor, grabbing a flashlight on the way to inspect me, splayed akimbo. I recall Tumor, a note of concern evident in his already-besotted voice, inquiring if they should gather me up and trundle me off to the nearest hospital. I was definitely conscious because I was rapidly becoming acquainted with an alarming host of anatomical maladies, from head down to knees, which had not been present mere seconds before. I managed to communicate to my comrades that the best thing they could do would be to prop me up, get me a drink of water, and leave me alone for a few minutes. Sure enough, some minutes later the toxic reaction—the extreme nausea leading up to this—slowly gave way to the now-pulsing, throbbing and in some locations, seeping contusions and abrasions, particularly along the left side of my body. By then, of course, I was able to determine that nothing significant was mangled or broken and, hence, that a run to the hospital was not imperative. And that I'd probably live to regret this day well into the future.

Under the harsh light of morning, I believe the tally was a very swollen and misshapen nose, especially at the bridge. Two black eyes. A swollen, cut, and bloody upper lip and 3 or 4 upper teeth quite sore, loose. A 3 to 4 inch-long gouge in the top of my head, very sensitive and just barely scabbed. Two or three neck vertebrae that alternated between sharp pain at the heretofore-normal-but-now-very-"wrong" movement of my head, and dull, constant ache. Bruised left elbow, ribs, knee, but especially, left hip, which felt like something broken. And badly mangled but not broken glasses, able to be straightened enough to see through driving back to the city a couple days later.

And the shirt; you shoulda seen the shirt! The cuffs, especially, were drenched in blood, stiff and slightly sticky. The sleeves and the front had blood rained on them, certainly from my nose, probably other sources as well. But even the sides and back had dull red splashes. We considered donating it to the Smithsonian—as testament to one man's battle against himself?— but after some discussion, thought better of it.

Moral

All right, so I ain't no Aesop, but doncha have to wonder about the notion of cosmic justice? I mean, in a fair world, don't we expect the good and the virtuous to be rewarded for their exemplary conduct, and the bad, corrupt, venal, and the greedy to be punished? Well, here I am, mere months after flirting with death, and all I've got is a moderate crick in my neck. True, my nose has a intriguing cant to it, but it functions normally. Then, there's an easily-felt 1 ½ x ¾" plowed scar on the top of my head, conveniently covered in hair. Basically recovered.

But a year and a half out, I've still got a buggered shoulder from having tried to keep a semblance of upper body fitness. The paradigm seems to work in opposite, at least in these instances. So much for the *ought to*s and the *should be*s.

I'll quit with a final news flash to teenagers everywhere (chronological or otherwise): Excessive intoxication, stripped of its prefixes and suffixes, is *toxic*. It may not be fatally toxic but, no mistake, it can and will hurt you. By succumbing to "Small River protocol," given my weakened condition, I had most assuredly poisoned myself and came very close to killing myself (breaking my neck, bleeding to death), as well. If such nice guys as Yers Truly can be brought so low by overindulgence, well, you know the old chestnut: *Forewarned*...

(April 2005)

Milestones

Coitus, gestation, birth,
Circumcision, baptism, inoculation,
Christening, quinceanera, bar mitzvah,
Prom, coronation, graduation,
Conscription, occupation, wedding,
Duet, ground breaking, house warming,
Tryst, denouement, duel,
Coup d'etat, abdication, trial,
Eviction, amputation, immolation,
Exorcism, stoning, execution,
Wake, funeral, cremation,
Absolution, resurrection, resolution

Tuna and the three bears

My first bear adventure was in Kashmir, on the outskirts of Srinagar, the Venice of the East. It was the summer of 1966, and it was still possible in those days for casual foreigners to travel there without getting held for ransom or killed in a border skirmish, though it was very much disputed territory between India and Pakistan even then. Of course traveling there meant surface transport over some pretty hairy roads, which is to say you were taking your life in your hands, anyway. Truth to tell, those roads probably killed more people, foreigners and locals alike, than all the military actions put together. Seasoned travelers tend to take for granted the inherent dangers of travel. There is no real travel experience without risk.

Shalimar Gardens, in Srinagar, were said to be the setting for Shangri-la, a centuries-old Persian paradise on earth. I hear it's a special place; I was there, but I don't remember it. I was already pretty wasted from the onset of hepatitis, though I didn't know it at the time. I was traveling with a fellow countryman, name of Mikhail—first generation native American of Russian émigrés, full head of thick, dark, curly hair and full beard, wiry build—who I met in Delhi. Since we were both headed in the same direction we traveled together for a while.

I had been traveling for at least the previous two months—ever since dropping through the Khyber Pass into Pakistan—into a hot, humid summertime soup, difficult for a foreign sojourner plunked into the severity of it to endure. Kashmir beckoned with higher elevations, tantalized with cool breezes and a respite from the thick, stultifying heat. Training to the end of the line, Jumma, in no particular hurry, we decided to

235

stay over a couple days in Amritsar, the Punjab's major city, and the Sikh's capital, home to their huge temple covered in gold leaf.

Within a day or two of arriving in Srinagar, we'd gotten lured into a "bear hunt." I don't know how we got suckered into the plan; like as not I was a little delirious from the onset of the illness. I knew I was off my normal pace, a condition I attributed to the long trip I'd endured in getting there—all day by bus—and the altitude: 8500 feet above sea level. Basically, these two Kashmiri salesmen presented the scenario where they would take us to a place where bears were regularly seen, they would provide us with rifles and point out the target. There was a modest fee-- $10 each?—we owed up front. If we shot the bear, we would owe another step up. Then, they were prepared to render the carcass in any way we might desire: preserve the hide and send it on? For a bite. The meat? Whatever you say, for a bite. For some strange reason, perhaps a fleeting lapse of rationality permitted us to indulge the fantasy of ourselves as bygone aristocratic travelers.

Me'm sab Buwana, big game hunter, slaughter mega-fauna around the world! The photos of previous bear hunters with their trophies were pretty enticing to a fairly weird mind-set. Which I guess we possessed at the time.

Our "guides" picked us up at 3:45 the next morning in order to take us to the bear hunting grounds before daylight. The ride consisted of the bed of a Datsun pickup. It was a half hour, maybe 40 minutes, of hanging on to the side of the truck to minimize the teeth rattling, butt hammering over the dirt roads. Finally we arrived at rural farmland in the foothills of the Srinagar basin. Corn appeared to be the crop in that vicinity. Five-foot-high stalks of ripening ears of corn drew bears down from the surrounding mountains, so the locals had concocted this scheme to sell the package to shoot the menace of their harvest, and make a few rupees in the process. Advance scouts had confirmed that a bear was indeed marauding the still very dark cornfield. We were to follow the guides out into the pre-dawn fields some few hundred yards and shoot this most recent intruder with the weapons at hand: WWI-vintage Lee-Enfield rifles, about ten pounds each.

By this time the allure and novelty of the experience had given way to a recognition of the absurdity, made embarrassingly clear when I couldn't keep up with the group: three or four of the locals, Mikhail and me. I felt so weak, so exhausted, that I was going to have to sit for a while and catch my breath. Mik might have been annoyed at the delay except he wasn't a lot more robust than me. For a brief period they debated *carrying* me, since the bear was not far away, but that's when I pulled the plug. It had been a weird enough proposition with any reflection. The need to be carried to the precise location where I could execute a practically set-up bear, all in order to show off somesort of trophy from the experience, was finally too much. I have a vague recollection of seeing a hint of some dark lump moving through the rows of corn in the first dim light—before retreating to the pickup and the trip back to the center of town.

Later that day, I believe, we got in to see a doctor in a local clinic, but by then it was obvious. Both of us had a noticeably tangerine pallor. The whites of my eyes were yellows. My urine was a bright orange; my liver was losing the ability to metabolize owing to this viral infection. We had *yellow jaundice*, or hepatitis A. The British doctor said there wasn't much he could do—no known medicine. We were to avoid alcohol, and fatty foods. We were to rest. Music to my ears!

I don't know the incubation period for hepatitis A, but if it's just a few days, then Amritsar was where Mikhail and I got exposed to it. From contaminated food, offered without cost to the people visiting or staying at the Gurudwara, or the utensils that came with the food, most likely. Other possibilities were mosquitos, and shared chillums, but we started showing symptoms within a day of each other. So if that incubation period was a week or more, it would have put our mutual exposure back in Delhi. I don't remember hanging out with Mikhail more than a day or two before we set out for Amritsar, another of those unanswerables.

We rented this houseboat on Dal Lake. For $2 each per day, we had private rooms on this catered houseboat, two western-style meals a day included! These meals were a special boon since we were not prepared to scout for decent restaurants in the vicinity, and lacked the skills, to say nothing of energy or patience to make our own meals. Furthermore, for the previous month or so I'd been hard pressed to find a meal that was not laced with fiery capsaicin, burning hot chilies, which I seemed to have a hard time getting used to. Now, breakfasts were toast, sometimes oatmeal, fruit, occasional eggs, and the ubiquitous sweetened milk tea. Late afternoon meals were chicken or lamb stews with carrots, onions, potatoes and other vegetables, sometimes rice. *Thas what ahm talkin 'bout!*

Hepatitis is a curious affliction. It wastes your body; I could barely drag myself to the bathroom. The doctor reported my weight at 120 lbs.; not since the 8th grade had I weighed so little. Those first two weeks I probably slept 16 or more hours a day. On the other hand, it leaves your mind alert and very much open to new possibilities. With nothing else to do and zero energy to do it, I found myself exploring ideas for hours on end. Also, I wrote my first short story, and read everything on the boat. It was a stone downer to be sick, as manifested in having no energy, but it was a mental picnic! Gradually, we regained our strength and by the end of a month, we were ready to get back on the road, back to Delhi before splitting up; me heading east to Lucknow, Varanasi, a detour back into the Himalayas to Kathmandu, return to Bodh Gaya, and Calcutta before flying on to Rangoon, then Bangkok and beyond.

Doubtless, that bear had but a few days' reprieve. His nightly depredations of that corn patch were numbered. Other tourists, aspiring Hemingways, would fall prey to the opportunity to bag their trophy. To this day, I remain grateful that I failed as a bear hunter in Kashmir. It was not to be my final opportunity.

* * * * *

Bear episode number two took place about a decade later on the Oregon Coast Range property my family and I shared with my brother and his growing family. While Pip was actively involved in building his house, his son at 16 months old was gaining confidence in walking, and exploring the forest opening immediately surrounding the building site.

I had recently acquired a bee hive from a one-legged bee keeper who owned some creek front property some three miles toward the mouth of the creek. As far as keeping bees went I was pretty much a rank amateur, but ol' man Larsen had talked me into the project. He gave me some literature on the subject, and provided me with the basic tools: gloves with sleeves that could be cinched tight against my forearms and a wide-brimmed pith helmet with a snug veil to keep angry bees from easy access to fleshy areas where they would happily sacrifice themselves by stinging me unmercifully for blundering through their home.

Unfortunately, I had to take possession of the hive before I had erected a bear-proof stand, a six-foot high platform, in the works but not yet completed. The only recourse for me was to position the hive on some boards a couple of feet off the ground at the base of the platform site for the day or two it would take me to complete construction of the stand. Well, the very night of placing the hive on its temporary location saw it torn into by a local bear, It was hard to blame him, who must have seen this windfall as manna from heaven. I was mightily upset, having to patch together the damaged hive boiling with belligerent bees, but Pip was more than a little traumatized. He and Linda needed to focus on home construction before the rains set in, and, short of hog tying my nephew—a wholly unworkable proposition—he was going to roam the area. However, a bear bold enough to raid a beehive some sixty yards from the work site in broad daylight posed a clear threat to their son. The kid would have made a tasty morsel to complement the honeycomb dessert! Thus, I faced the heavy irony of my Buddhist, vegetarian, peace/ love/nonviolent brother lobbying me to remove this threat by shooting the bear.

I borrowed a single fire thirty-aught-six deer rifle with a handful of bullets from "Mayor" Tom Smith, a neighbor up the coast a ways. We parked my pickup truck facing the hive and staked out the crime scene as evening descended. Sure enough, with the fading light, Barry Bear showed up for a second helping of my nascent apiary. I took careful aim at the dark movement in the darkness and took a shot from the cab of the pickup. An explosion of light and sound. A conspicuous kick in the shoulder, as well. All for… Nothing! With blazing flashlights searching the vicinity, there was no bear, no sign of blood. But just maybe we'd discouraged him from hanging around…

Ha! On the following morning's inspection, Mr. Ursus had paid another visit to the hive and once again I had to cobble together a makeshift repair to the damaged hive frames. *Now, that's just arrogance, to hit me again!,* I was thinking as I patched up their home for the day. After dark, when all the worker bees had returned, my plan was to close up the entrance and transport the hive three miles down creek to Larson's place. See, the rule of hive movement, as I learned it, is *Three feet or three miles*. Which means, if you must relocate a hive, move it up to three feet, or at least three miles, or the bees, with their highly specialized sense of navigation, would not be able to find their way back home. Move it 100 feet or half a mile and you've condemned all those workers—on a late spring day, thousands of them—to be abandoned, lost. Before I could return in the evening to move it, Barry had beat me to it.

So for a second night, we lay siege to the hive. We may have gotten a little closer that second night—perhaps 30, 35 yards—but with the same results. About the time Pip was dozing off I shot at a less than distinct movement in the gloom with nothing to show for it. I was starting to think this bear was, aside from stubborn and won't-take-no-for-an-answer, bullet proof. Still, humility dictates the possibility my aim was skewed by fatigue from the day's work, a silent hour of strained concentration on the hive site, and that joint we might've smoked to prepare us for the stake out.

Night three, no more Mr. Nice Guy. Forego the logic that a single bullet striking anywhere over a fairly large portion of the bear's outline would be fatal. That presupposed you could hit the bear. Accept the logic that the dispersion of a handful of pellets—buck shot from a 12 gauge shotgun—have a better chance of hitting the bear. For the third time I fired a gun at this bear, and for the third time he ran away. I was demoralized. Except he didn't seem to come back. Perhaps he'd gotten the message: He was to leave us alone. Leave my bees alone, and by implication, quit menacing the kids, and I'd stop trying to kill him.

About a week later, another coastie, Gentleman Jim Bowers, was up creek for a visit. We were traipsing around on a warm summer day when Jim picked up the smell of carrion. We made a short search, our noses drawing us ever closer, and 150 yards off in the dense brush of the Coast Range rain forest we found his carcass. He was a mature boar with a fist-sized hole in his side that must have taken most of the blast of my 12 gauge. He might have been 200 pounds, and there was no convenient way to move him in this stage of decomposition, so we decided to dig a hole next to the carcass and roll him in. This we did, but not before harvesting the 20 claws. The rest of him was putrefying. We had the sense to mark the grave to retrieve the skull and bones after a couple of years. To this day, I've got his skull and a femur or two adding a little rustic charm to my nearby cabin.

As a brief aside, I'll mention a tale of serendipity concerning the journey of my ten bear claws, my half of the macabre harvest. Several unrelated events came together, with very little expense or effort on my part—aside from having to shoot the bear in the first place—to create a rather striking bear claw necklace. Evidence of the resourcefulness of the underground economy.

1) For a previous birthday, my wife had found a small collection of what looked like handmade, low-fired, clay beads.

2) A coastie/refugee from Eugene I knew was a pretty good silversmith, and coincidentally fond of reefer. Furthermore,

3) I knew some folks who grew a little wacky weed and owed me a favor. It was easy for me to finagle a pound or so of minor leaf mixed with tiny buds.

4) In exchange, Jackie capped all the claws and mounted turquoise on the two biggest ones using silver and turq she provided. I think I drilled another turquoise nugget to serve as a center piece, then I strung it on monofilament fishing line.

Voila! A necklace with gravitas (see back cover photo).

* * * * *

My third noteworthy bear experience happened in the late spring or early summer of 1984, when I was by myself at my Oregon Coast Range cabin. The rest of my family were living in Paisley, and I was living most of those months in McMinnville working in the vineyards and orchards of the Sokol-Blosser Winery. It was a temporary job that paid pretty well for grunt work, but the real draw was the camaraderie I shared with my fellow warriors in the trenches: Jamie, Ben, Terry, and the two Lindas.

I got back to my Coast Range digs when I could carve out a couple of consecutive days free, and this was a slow phase of summer, in the build up to *crush*, the intense fall harvest time when all the grapes get pressed to juice, and in short order, on their way toward becoming wines.

One of the first things I do up creek after a long absence is to slough off the city pace by taking a leisurely walk around the perimeter of my meadow. On this particular perambulation I noticed an abundance of bear scat here and there. Somebody had made himself at home in my periods of absence. I didn't pay it further attention until the next morning, first light, when I was awakened by noisy snuffling around my back door, less than three feet from my head, lying on my left side, facing the door.

The bed dominates that room. Its head sits against the north wall. Anyone—or *anything*—entering from the back door, in the east wall northeast corner, would have to walk around the foot of the bed to arrive in the living room, through the bathroom. This door has four glass panes occupying the center of the door above the knob. I always sleep on the side of the bed facing the back door. One final factoid having no particular significance one way or another: If I take a shower before going to bed, as I had that night, I invariably sleep in the altogether, unconstrained by enclosing garments.

Even without glasses that morning, once I realized what was making the sound, I let out a blood-curdling shriek, threw off the sleeping bag, and leapt out of bed, bellowing my head off, reeling off a string of blasphemies, profane imprecations, and otherwise wholly undignified verbal abuse of this bear and all his skulking ursine relatives. It's fair to say, this sudden explosive outburst startled the bear, who drew back a few steps. I didn't really have a plan, going on guts more than anything, but by snatching open the door and running out flailing my arms, thundering at the top of my lungs, I'd seized the momentum. Mr. Bear decided to exercise caution in dealing with this lunatic, and made a discreet withdrawal up the hill toward the tree line.

It was a summer morning without rain, but still dewy-wet and chilly. I might have taken a step or two off the brick poach to reinforce the bear's flight, but not more. It wouldn't do to press the point too far and have Mr. Bear call my bluff. I'd gotten away with it initially. Did I want to push my luck? Sr. Oso could have stopped bolting for the trees; he could've turned to face me—my nekkid, pink, effectively hairless self already starting to get goose bumps from the chill…

That single, spontaneous event might have ended differently. As it turned out, I was doubly heartened to have had the experience of defending my home—in my birthday suit— against a hungry and curious bear with nothing more than bluster.

Moral value ethics

This is as much a request from a perceived oppositional position—the dialectic perspective will soon become apparent— as it is an expression of a point of view. I want to talk about morals and values. I've encountered a lot of commentary among Christian spokespersons and, often, Republican politicians about the preservation or defense of "moral values." Aren't all moral concerns values? Is it meaningful to say there's an important difference between morals and values?

If they're pretty much synonymous, does it serve another purpose to double up the terms? I'm wondering if the phrases *value morals,* or *moral values* pack a bigger wallop, semantically speaking, than values or morals by themselves. A hierarchy of value morals, as in some moral values are qualitatively better, or more important than others, perhaps?

The context of value morals, interestingly enough, invariably includes a strong stance on the abortion and homosexual issues. I understand that these are very important positions to defend for a great many people; furthermore, that morals and/or values are *essential* to an understanding and an orientation toward these human acts. What I don't understand is the enormous amount of attention/ consternation brought to bear on these and few other concerns, while for sheer scale of value-moral issues, they would seem to be dwarfed by the likes of global poverty; climate change; the vastly disproportionate distribution of wealth; ongoing race/class/gender discrimination; five(?) years-and-counting, hundreds of thousands killed, two million displaced, in the unending tragedy in Darfur—you choose. Are you saying that these issues, and others, don't rise to the level of *moral values*?

If *every (human) life is precious,* every zygote, wanted or not, wouldn't we get more bang for our money, attention, and time if we, say, helped provide complete anti-malarial medicines for all the globally afflicted? While we're at it, let's throw in HIV/AIDS meds for the African Continent (completely doable if we'd back off outright killing or threatening to kill citizens of various cultural entities in the Middle East). Hell, pick your human tragedy; virtually any chronic global disaster deserves a better response, morally/ ethically speaking, wouldn't you say?

So I ask America's Christian Conservatives, and Republicans in general, where's the perspective? By any moral measure, how could one justify preoccupation with "murder of the unborn"—on a scale of suffering by the numbers, easily 10,000 to one—that's *millions* of people whose suffering we could at least reduce/mitigate, if not outright eliminate from one of the afore-cited disasters, compared to mere *thousands* of American abortions annually? It just does not compute, morally or ethically speaking.

And what is up with the pathological preoccupation with mutual buggery between consenting adult males, or women having sex with other women? Granted, it won't be the same physiology of sex, anatomically speaking, as in a stereotypical heterosexual relationship, but why do you care? Just reading/hearing the words make you recoil, right? Why should that threaten you *so* much? It's part of human behavior; it doesn't have to be part of *your* behavior. Your Lord will sit in judgment, so who're you to play God?

It is the worst of smells, the stench of elitist bigotry. Xenophobic, homophobic, ethnocentric hypocrisy.

(2008)

The sole constant

The indeterminate default for everything
non-personal, non-specific third person
singular subject pronoun   It
keeps changing. All of it
always does. To assume otherwise
would be an illusion. And to forget
that it does   keep changing
though You are not an it
is to cease being

                        F

                            r

                                e

                                    e

                                        e

                                            e

                                                    !

                                                        ?

                                                            !

The rooster, imperiled

At the ripe old age of 63, I've today experienced a "first." And *last*, is my fervent hope: I caught a small portion of the head of my little red rooster in my fly.

Funny how quickly one's attention can shift. One moment a person can be deep into cogitating the eternal verities and in a blinding flash all thoughts are banished, all consciousness is focused, laser-like, on a miniscule patch of anatomy. The hands, unimpeded by thought, swiftly move to reverse the process in hopes of disengaging rent flesh from interlocking teeth in steel jaws—which they succeeded in doing. Oh, my!

Fortunately, I don't expect... (Ack! What object pronoun should I choose: *him, it,* or *me*?—a bona fide linguistic, existential dilemma) to be more than temporarily out of action. This rooster will crow again; *Xristos Anesti!* Who knows? In a lull in the conversation someday, I might even get to trot 'im out as evidence of an old war wound.

(Summer 2004)

Pip's *Kanreki*

You know, I don't circulate much in socially-representative groups—for all I know spiritual folks are a dime a dozen out there. But it seems to me that my brother, Pip, is a rare one: a person who radiates spirituality without having to talk it to death. One who is able to walk the walk. And while it's been an amazing ride so far, you can't help but marvel at how two guys raised together—same environment, same parents, same influences—could have produced such different results. On the one hand, a pure and creative soul. On the other, me, a brother significantly shy of the mark. A speculation or two are in order.

When we were growing up, little brother was unresponsive to my carefully planned tutelage, and corrective measures were often required. I noted from an early age a resistant and defiant streak despite my best efforts at imposing humane negative reinforcement. Growing up on the outskirts of Phoenix, AZ, summers were even then hot, and we'd seek refuge in the nearby community swimming pool. One of the games we invented to amuse ourselves was "Taxi," a harmless pastime in which we took turns giving each other piggy-back rides in the pool. Bodies are, of course, far more buoyant in water so Pip had little trouble maneuvering in water with me positioned on his back. The rider *drove* the taxi by gripping the ears and aiming the face in the direction he wanted to go, which was sooner-than-later toward the deep end of the pool. The game usually ended (prematurely, I should add) with a lot of dramatic "taxi engine" sputtering and disparaging comments as to my instructional intentions.

A scant two years separate us but in our younger years I'd have to say the gulf between us seemed greater to me than to Pip. It seemed to me, however, there was a defining moment that united us in common cause. Pip has a variation of this story but it bears repeating: A lot of you younger whipper-snappers think that rock'n'roll has been around forever. Not so. And I'm here to disabuse a few misguided souls that imagine the advent of rock was signaled by the appearance of Kiss, or perhaps Toto, or their ilk. The year I went off to high school, 1955, heralded the emergence of the true rock'n'roll elders. The pantheon of Chuck Berry, Fats Domino, Bo Didley, Elvis, Jerry Lee Lewis, and a host of bit players slammed a crowbar into the standard way young people evaluated music. Right there at the center of the maelstrom was Dickie Penniman, *aka* Little Richard.

To this day I can't make out half what he sings, shouts, or screams but it's clear the lyrics aren't the point. To a teenager in 1955, hearing the Georgia Peach for the first time on the radio, *understanding* the music was irrelevant. This was not a cognitive experience at all; far from it. With Little Richard's first irrepressible shriek, an aural jolt he artfully festooned all his early hits with, if you weren't stone deaf you felt a sudden lightning bolt to the bowels (or was it gonads?)—and popular music was transformed forevermore.

From unsuspecting parents, on the occasion of obligatory present exchanges, we had finagled a crude—by modern standards—45 rpm record player. What it lacked in tone fidelity we compensated for with volume. (Some would argue, *over-*compensated, but that's neither here nor there.) And you know

251

the rest of the story, right? Because it's been played out in countless homes over the generations since. Sputtering and apoplectic parents all over the nation, unaccustomed to such bestial and unholy *noise,* demanded its immediate cessation with perhaps something familiar and soothing in its place: in our day that was Guy Lombardo, Perry Como and Dean Martin (the crooners); Doris Day, Patti Page, or Rosemary Clooney.

It was at such a time that a kind of epiphany occurred. Suddenly this obnoxious upstart of a little brother was an ally against the power-clutching ogres; an emergent Machiavelli began to assert itself. We were *both equally* subjected to a wholly unjustified discrimination. And of course, anything that drew us together against the common enemy, itself, developed the aura of sacredness. (For those of you yearning for a hint of the magic of Little Richard, a complimentary airing is in order.)

Besides music, traveling figures prominently in our relationship. We canned Green Giant peas together in Waitsburg, Washington, in the summer of '63. Then, in the fall, we took a miserable 2nd class train from the border town of Nogales to Mexico City, with stops at Mazatlan and Guadalajara along the way. In the center of Mexico City, Alameda Park, where we'd go to sip a little rot-gut tequila and hang out, I remember the hustlers and shoeshine boys calling us *Existentialistas.* This was pre-pre-pre-hippie days, and I'm still not sure what they meant, but we bore the epithet proudly.

Fast forward to Siphnos, an Aegean island where Pip, Vernette, and I rented a small house ($13 for the month) in the winter of '65. The village bread seller would comb the neighborhood in the early morning calling *"psomii!"* We'd hear him approaching a couple of narrow streets over and 15 minutes before he got to us—time enough to throw on clothes and grab some change. Fresh, still-warm bread delivered to your doorstep on the back of a donkey; there are worse ways to start the day.

Forward again to China in the spring of '86. China in the days of Deng Xiaoping and Tourist Money, which you had to buy and were supposed to spend in designated places, but could exchange at considerable advantage on the black market for *Renmenbi*s (people's money). Hong Kong to Guangzhou by train. Then a two-day boat ride up the Pearl River by glorified deck class. "Blame It on the Bossa Nova" in Chinese, over and over, until a corps of foreigners mutinied, took over the ship's sound system, and plied the rest of the journey with Supertramp's "Breakfast in America." Yang Shuo, the artist and Beatnik capital of the People's Republic. The memories keep folding in on themselves.

Strange journeys of another stripe include the Yellow Submarine (*"everyone of us is all we need"*), our communal experience and a story unto itself (see "Voyage of the Yellow Submarine," authored by Pip and me, and a few other survivors), and the important alliance we continue to share in having co-owned 50 + acres for the last 27 years. Pip, I am fortunate and honored to be your brother. You are an inspiration to me and a rock-solid partner. Happy 60th Birthday!

Let me say in closing, since this is considered to be a mixed and polite assemblage, for those of you more interested in Pip's "checkered," if not lurid and felonious past see me afterwards for details…

(Presented to +/- 20 people at our Mt Tabor home on the occasion of my brother's *Kanreki*, or 60th birthday; that's five times around the 12-year zodiac cycle: 6/03)

Failing Dennis

Well, the forces of Corporatocracy have won again. It was a stacked deck to begin with, but the little guy had the heart, courage, and the will to try to make America better—*again!* (Yes, he faced the same fate four years ago in 2004.) He fought the good fight. He didn't fail us; *we* failed him.

"What do you mean *we*," you say, "and how did we fail him?" The *we* who believe we should never have gotten embroiled in Iraq failed him. The *we* who wanted America's Imperial forces out of Iraq in 2004, and still want them out now, failed him. Americans who believe the most cost-effective way for a civilized society to care for its medically needy is by a national, single-payer health care system failed him. Those of us who have come to see that such treaties as NAFTA and the WTO are rigged on behalf of corporate stakeholders, at the expense of feudal labor in emerging economies, and the environment everywhere—we failed him.

The beacon of *government by the people, for the people* is a little dimmer today without Dennis Kucinich in the race for president.

(an unpublished Letter to the Editor, *Oregonian*, 1/25/08, in response to news that Dennis Kucinich was dropping out of the presidential race)

Ostreona, Queen of Mollusca

I love the morning oyster
       in her moist and drowsy sleep
She often beckons to me
       nestled in her nether deep

Reluctant to arousal
       after torpid night of dreams
Slowly she awakens
       to the gentle prod and seems

to flutter all a-tremble
       not quite ready to begin
Perhaps a trifle angry
       at intrusion thrust within

And of the sultry afternoon
       what rapture shall we play
The dulcet chords of paradise
       commence the matinee!

But wait! What of the evening
       while the vespers sweetly toll?
In the cautious creep of twilight
       don't you miss your jellyroll?

In the fading light of eventide
      a-cloistered in her lair
'tis a haven in the valley,
      a sanctum without care

And in the starry firmament
      her majesty, the moon,
offers coy encouragement
      to punctuate the gloom

Embrace the evening oyster
      in her darkened citadel
with your poised and ready clapper
      proudly ring her bell

Yea, all the hours of the day,
      every season, every clime
Just to nuzzle the juicy oyster
      is a passion quite sublime!

(Spring 1995)

The semantics of reality

One colleague wants to teach fact vs. opinion to her students. Another thinks to further parse opinion from "informed" opinion, whatever that may be. On the one hand, not having my dictionary within reach, I'd say opinion is belief without *adequate* or *thorough* substantiation. So informed opinion is, I take it, an interpretation based on *some* evidence, a decidedly relative position. And one who possesses an informed opinion is somewhat knowledgeable on the subject? Then, what's an *expert*; one who knows *very much* about the issue? Because we can't really be expected to know everything there is to know about a subject, can we? That's one of the attributes we ascribe to the "Almighty"—Omniscience, all-knowing. On the other hand, what do we really mean by *fact*?

For a different take on the matter, consider *objective* reality, e.g., "Common, unadulterated, fresh water at sea level freezes at 0 degrees C., 32 F." Note the necessity of some hedges even with this statement. We can't just say water freezes at 32F, 0C, since sea water doesn't freeze at 32F, and fresh water doesn't freeze at 0C at 3000m altitude.

Subjective reality, the counterpart in this dichotomy, is everything *not* pinned down by hard, empirical evidence, replicable every time; everything not locked away in the mostly physics, chemistry, or mathematics domain (until you consider Heisenberg, of course). Conceivably, someone could question whether it is "real" if it is not universal or objectifiable. Most would counter that the pain from a sprained ankle, bruised shoulder, burned finger, or headache (name your malady) is real enough to *me*, the experiencer. Subjective reality, in terms of communicable meaning, or feeling, requires *negotiation.*

We get to, or have to (depending on your perspective), come to *some* sort of agreement on meaning in all things human. Any more, most of those agreements (thankfully) are negotiated via language—all the *humane* accords are achieved via language and not clubs or arrows, "smart" bombs or toxic biota. The best means we seem to have come up with so far is "agreement" by consent via the vote, majority rule. And while many of us, as members of a minority, at any given time suffer the yoke of the agreement of the marginal majority, we endure it because it is at least not arbitrarily imposed; not egregiously unfair.

Call me a stickler for semantic accuracy, but if we aren't scrupulous in our efforts to say as precisely as possible what we mean *as individuals*, then how can we hope to concur on abstractions of social policy, ethics, laws and scofflaws, and/or aesthetics, *collectively*?

Or, in brief, if we don't say what we mean, how can we possibly mean what we say?

(Spring 2002)

Quandary

My wife whimpers in her sleep
sometimes mumbles unintelligible
anxieties. I want to hold her, guard her
from the demons, but these adversaries are
beyond my protection. Outside/inside
my defenses. Should I wake her, tell her
that everything's alright? That our bed,
this room, the night are as usual? Or let her
struggle, fitful, hoping she will resolve
her plight, cast out her demons, and emerge
perhaps bruised but undaunted from this
task of living?

(January 2008)

Part Five

Grackle's reckoning

The scene shifts away from the central preoccupation of Grackle Pisswing—the looming biospheric catastrophe—to imagery that swings back and forth from un- or sub-consciousness to alert, rational consciousness. Night approaches, but in the fading light three ancient figures are seen engaged in a task as if bound by duty. They are wizened crones, but in the gathering eventide gloom they might just as well be giant spiders huddled together, given their activity.

One seems to have ceased, or slowed down, spinning an elaborate and extensive cord. Said cord displays different textures, abrasions, even girth and color variations along its length, from which we could infer varied use. Rough and abraded here, while sleek and sinewy elsewhere, in its own way it tells a story not unlike the *quipu,* the Incan string-recording device, their "writing" system.

The second apparition, in satisfaction, occupies herself measuring this latest accreted cord, determining its length; eight legs make for light work! The third old hag prepares her shears—mandibles serve nicely—for the act of cutting the cord, according to the established calculation. There is no malice, no joy nor regret, in this coordinated act. They perform with practiced hands—or is it segmented limbs?—having acted out this ritual since time immemorial. As inexorable as the sunrise signals the morning, and sunset announces the coming night, Birth foretells Death. It's not personal with Clotho, Lachesis, and Atropos, the *Moirai* or Fates; they have a job to do and they accomplish it with grim efficiency. There are no exceptions.

As of this writing, this enactment is not yet center stage for Grackle. It's on the periphery, only occasionally discernible in the shadows, as if the actors were performing a practice run. On the edge, in and out of awareness, as a reminder. The final calculation has not been made; the lifeline is still attached, the very antithesis of the severed umbilical cord at the outset of a new-born-baby's life.

Just a wink and a nod and a sly leer from the harpies across the gulf, a reminder while the cord pays out still more, to stay focused on what is "important" in life—value, meaning, beauty and relevance—because many indicators here and there tell Grackle Pisswing he is well along in his final phase.

A modest consideration of meaning and relevance yielded *purpose*—regarding life in general, but his own in particular. Our cosmically disoriented, existential, hairless ape would tell you that, with the exception of the occasions when he succumbed to self-indulgence and self-serving, he'd spent most of his rational life trying to distill purpose and meaning out of experience. One would think these decades of even desultory research would have yielded somesort of findings to these reflections. Dare we inquire about *results*? They would be modest and limited in scope, of course. Tentative and subjective, unavoidably. Alas, no such tidy set of conclusions seem to be forthcoming.

Then, if not the Who, the What: Corporally at minimum, a lumpy, 175-pound bag of amino acids, specifically the nucleotides comprising the DNA of all life: adenine, cytosine, guanine, and thymine (A, C, G, and T), that conspire to foster, then sustain life through the delicate but critical interaction of several biochemical systems. For a while. Whatever the reach of the arc, however, life is *the* miracle. Made more remarkable by a degree of self-awareness, and now and then, a spark of passion. That, and the fact that this particular bag demonstrates the ability to "bark" out of both ends.

Ultimately, you have to let it go.
One way or another we are all going to let go
the panoply of unfair situations, injustices,
and power disparities that contribute to the pain
and suffering of our fellow humans. Let it go.
Our scramble to consume the last of the easily gotten
fossil fuels, and the attendant carbon consequences.
Let it go. Social disequivalencies/unproportionalities
have existed since humans settled into communities.
Even before. Tragedy, the antipode of joy,
is drearily commonplace; let it go.
It is only in the last generation that awareness
of human impact on the environment
has taken on the stature of a moral imperative.
Yet in the end, one's individual efforts
are largely inconsequential, and surely only folly
would lead one to expect otherwise, no matter
how eloquent. Meanwhile, you are just another
consumer-polluter, contributing en masse
to the coming Unravelling.
Let it go.

We leave our tottering protagonist here, ill at ease, dazed, at war with himself, grappling with his lot,

though significantly self-induced,

on the gyrating meat-wheel,

villering, klopfustenating

in strepatulous conipetence.

GTC GGG CCC GGT CAG TAC TTG GAT GGG TGA CCG CCT ATG AAC ACC GGG TGC TGT TGG ATG CAG TGG CGG AAT CTG AGG TCG GGC TAG CCC CTT CCT TGC CGA GGT ATG AAG TAA GCG ACG TGG CCA AAT GCC GAC AGG TCC GTC TTA CCG GCG GAT TTC TGT CGG AGC TTG AAG TGC CCT ATG CAA TTC GGG ACA TCA GGT CTG AGG TGT CGC ACC TAA GGC CGT GGA TGA CAC GTT ACG TCT ATC CCT CCG ATA GCA TTC CTG GAT GCC AAG GTT CGA TGC GGT CAG TGA CCG TTG GCG TGA ATA GTC GTT ACG CGA AGC TTA ATT CAC ACT…

Animus

Virtually anyone past childhood has some notion of death if only that, at some point, all people cease to be. This translates into curiosity at minimum and, for many, varying degrees of fear additionally. Since no one living can wholly, truly know what death is we are left with "not life." The old paradigm of "All things are either A or Not-A" doesn't tell us much. The archetype of the *other*.

So naturally, the history of mankind (which is nothing if not the narration of the human story) is replete with speculation from various quarters throughout the ages as to what constitutes the afterlife—and, for that matter, the before-life as well. Hence, we've got the range of mystical/spiritual interpretations, more often than not with ethical injunctions attached to one's conduct in life in order to safeguard favorable treatment, and avoid punishment in the hereafter, i.e. *Religion*. It is, furthermore, beyond dispute that huge numbers of humanity have found solace and consolation from religious rituals and ceremonies. The fact that some of these precepts have been around hundreds, if not thousands, of years seems to increase the comfort and credibility; hoary dogma seems to enjoy a greater level of satisfaction than the newly coined ones.

There appears to be, in addition to the natural yin/yang, duality, dichotomy of life-death, the same concept with good/bad. Needless to say, depending on which culture or which age as reference, there has been due attention paid to the extremes, the polar opposites, as opposed to the emphasis placed on the means, expressed by Thomas Wolfe, "The minute-winning days, like flies, buzz home to death and each moment is a window on all time" (*Look Homeward, Angel*).

But most of us don't find ourselves spending much time in those extremes. In my experience, it's the space/time *between* the poles, the interstices that occupy the bulk of our lives. Those rare occasions when pure, undistilled "Right" is knowable *and known,* can give you goose bumps and raise the hair on the back of your neck (vestiges of our feral selves?), to say nothing of being humbling, and/or frightening. In the day-to-day reality, however, the gradations, the continuum of options, the spectral facets of perspective, context, and validity make every event a negotiable occasion. For everyone who has a stake in the outcome of the negotiation. Zen suggests that we are both poles in the dichotomy. And everything in between.

(Portland 1996)

Tom Emmens, RIP

Thomas, you red-bearded pirate! You ol' libertine!
Freebooter! Thank you for this
bittersweet opportunity to reflect on your life,
to learn how to die. To pull together
by the loss of a loved one, a community that you
defined. To thank you for sharing your graceful life
with me. You pretty much ripped through life
on your terms. Like no one else in my experience,
you finessed temporary jobs
alternating with unemployment compensation
and plied the scheme over *decades*. I was in awe.

But the wages of sin *and* virtue catch up with us all
in the end; I just didn't think them nasty ol' wages
would snag you quite so quickly. Maybe you'd been
fending off the Final Comeuppance for a while—
who isn't?—but I was selfish, thinking,
We'll have more good times together.
I missed our face-to-face goodbyes and now
this will have to do. So it's not so much *Goodbye*
as *Good journey*: an appreciation of the one
you've completed and a salute
to the one you've just begun.

(June 2005)

On learning

Learning seems to be made up of active and passive aspects. Perhaps the best example of an active, systematized learning process, i.e., learning on an instructional basis, is a society's educational systems. Virtually all of us have had first-hand experience with the externally directed, "formal" education of the school curriculum. Most of us were required (by parents and society's expectations; hence the intentionality, *their* intentions) to attend interminable years of teacher-fronted, regimented curricula. If we wanted to advance to the next level of achievement—and appease our social milieu—we took the necessary steps, at least some of the time enduring, if not resenting, the process. This set of experiences perhaps best exemplifies active education. Thus, in an active environment, we have people who attend to learn (the students), a setting in which learning may take place (the classroom), and a professional trained to present the formalized curriculum (the teacher).

It is generally agreed that younger members of society lack the awareness of society's needs and expectations in order to seek out on their own the education necessary to prepare them for a healthy, successful integration into society. Additionally, most parents these days are occupied with their livelihoods, such that they lack the time and expertise to adequately educate their children. Hence, the systematized public and private schools and their educators, presumably trained to optimize this task.

This highlights the importance of the *relationship* between the teacher and students, only less so the relationship of the teacher and the subject matter. Every student recognizes, after a few years of classes, that there are good (*e.g.*, interesting, stimulating, and provocative) teachers and not-so-good teachers. Likewise, it takes very few years of teaching experience to recognize that some students are eager—or at least willing—to learn, while others build obstacles, real or imagined, to prevent or minimize learning. Extrapolating this notion, we could say the best prepared, most gifted teacher cannot reach the student adamantly unwilling to learn; the adage, *You can lead a horse to water but can't make it drink*, comes to mind. However, a highly-motivated teacher, willing and flexible enough to try different approaches to reach initially-resistant students surely communicates something, even if it eludes students' test results.

As we get older, though, we come to recognize another aspect of learning, namely, a passive form. Passive learning occurs all the time, often unconsciously. This occurs, in its most basic form, in stimulus/response, real-life experience. One learns to respect fire (and by extension, hot things) by experiencing the pain of being burned—usually one lesson is enough! With hunger, one learns to seek out things to eat, and so on. In less physiological S-R terms, we may perceive that an individual's inquiry yields benefits and, as a result, s/he may be willing to search the various sources of information that will fulfill that knowledge need.

In active, as well as passive learning, the key term seems to be *motivation*—or lack thereof. How does a high school student, or otherwise not-yet-fully-mature adult, become motivated to learn what the schools, and ultimately the society, expect of him/her? How does a school system (via its agents, the teachers) coax, encourage, entice, cajole, and persuade the student to take education seriously, when the student has only a vague appreciation for the application of the subject matter to his/her life, and questions the relevance of the entire system? This, while the educational environment, including the teachers themselves, often miss the mark, in terms of presenting a meaningful correlation of subject matter to students' lives.

Motivation, self- or externally imposed, is intrinsically tied to the recognition of *relevance* to one's life, if not in the present, then in some presumed future connection.

Chance

One life, one chance
with your flash of spark
to kindle a flame and warm others,
to pool with others a little light.
Soon enough a new tide rushes in
sweeping away all in its reach.
That scudding flame is doused
forever, the wisp of smoke
lost in the breeze.
One chance!

Brain farts

*How can one lead if others will not follow? And if no one will follow, well then, we've got pure anarchy!

*A man can live on hope. Decidedly not very healthily for very long, but hope can sustain a person for a while. Without hope being nurtured or reinforced in some way, however, you cannot live. We're not talking about the body, now; that you can keep alive with beans and rice and very little else. It's keeping the heart and soul alive, and for that we need to serve up a different repast.

Hope of what, you ask? For me, hope is fed by fantasy, but if the hope isn't from time to time at least partially lived out in somesort of real-life interaction, then the fantasies wither and are shed finally, as the vine gives up its leaves and shrivels in winter; as in old age. Some people's hope is rooted in a lust for personal gain. I'm a curious beast because while I decry as ignoble the glorification of Mammon, I pay homage to another, equally base deity. The *succubae* dominate my fantasies. (early '80s)

*Ever the wedge, never the glue

*Little or no government *by* the people insures, sooner or later, government will not be *for* the people, either. Government not for the majority of the people is, QED, government for the few at the expense of the many. Such a government can no longer maintain the pretext of a representative democracy.

*what to eat   what to drink
who to fuck   what to think
Always the question   always the choice
Never the answer but always the voice

* A philosophical question: Is a condition or state of being less valuable or important because it occurs effortlessly? Without a studied, practiced approach? Some would say all the important lessons occur when pain is experienced directly. Consider love—in any of its manifestations, but especially sexual love. If it happens too quickly, without somesort of requisite duet (or is it duel?) of shared experience, then it is held to be cheap, lacking in meaning, inconsequential (except in the event of pregnancy, or STDs). As if that initial experience couldn't build into one of greater depth as shared time allowed; there has to be a beginning point to any relationship.

I hated the long, drawn-out, ritualistic courtships in my young adulthood. Such initiations, rites of passage, used to drive me crazy. Sex was such a big hurdle for me that I wanted to establish that degree of intimacy early on. And it almost never happened that way—due to my failure in persuasive abilities? Four eyes and acne? Pheromones on the back burner? A chemically skewed libido? Whatever the reason(s), said condition was the bane of my high school and my early college years.

  * 'e couldn't when 'e ortn't
  so 'e tupped 'er when 'e did.

  *A major concern of mine is that I will be judged merely as a wordsmith, a philologist—that is to say, one who is good at word use. Whereas the real goal/desire is to be thought of as good with words, strung together in sentences and paragraphs in coherent, meaningful discourse about issues of social significance.

  Is that asking too much?

  Two wrongs don't make a right, goes the adage. Ah, but consider: Three rights *do* make a left!

  *In the last two rounds, Adam, a somewhat schizoid hominid loses a game of computer hearts, a game he'd led up until this endpoint, come-from-behind victory on the part of Pauline, the computer-generated droid on the left. *In the last two rounds,* Adam mutters to himself. He briefly contemplates playing another game when his uncle, Walter Eagle, having watched all this, interjects, *Whadya trying to do, change the outcome?*

Not change, Adam answers, after some thought. *Recontextualize, would be more like it...*

*Since one cannot defer pain—anticipation of a painful event is itself compelling pain—does it follow that one cannot defer pleasure, either?

*Ken Kesey, one of my psychic and literary mentors, knew a few things about the human condition. He said in different ways on different occasions, when confronted with overwhelming and unrelenting adversaries, we need to mock 'em. Poke fun at their stodgy, cheerless, mechanistic plodding. Make fun of them any way we can. Let ridicule be our ally. Bring on the humor. And in so doing, of course, we make fools of ourselves.

Since we are all patently, blatantly fools in so many ways, an acknowledgment of this reality, a small portion of humble pie, is not such a terrible thing. May it restore our humanity in the recognition of our fallibility.

*Wishes to ashes, lust to rust
walk if you want to, run if you must

*Let us agree to not call them "leaders" anymore. It's inaccurate and it gives the wrong impression. We should reject the notion that we need to be led. Let's call them what they were elected to be: *our representatives*, however poorly they may perform that role. S/he was elected to represent our interests, but the tendency is for our representatives to respond to inducements of the moneyed interests, via *their* representatives, the lobbyists, rather than the interests of the public.

Let's further agree that our experiment in self-governance is going to take more involvement than begrudgingly submitting to taxation and voting every two to four years, if we want it to survive. *Ah, but what manner of "additional involvement" is envisioned?* you ask. Clearly, one thing we can do is to inform our elected officials in no uncertain terms that they work for us. *We the people* are the leaders; they are to follow our lead, our instructions. They are to represent our wishes in Congress, nothing more or less... *Or?*

> *I got the key to yo' lock
> gots the love of yo' life
> down deep where you live
> I got to make you my wife.

*Realizing that I am as guilty as the next person for seeking intellectual shortcuts / dichotomies (e.g., liberal / conservative; Republican / Democrat; pro-development / pro-preservation of the environment)—even recognizing my own predilection to fall prey to such patterns, I eschew, to the extent I can, the notion of labeling. I don't want to be pigeonholed by some one-size-fits-all label that is supposed to capture the entire range of my thoughts/feelings on a subject, so my default set is to treat each individual based on his/her presentation, and not as somesort of category.

*The Kitty Blues

It's a hard life!
How many ways can you sing this song?
Woe is me, life is so hard!
The plaintive cry of our aged old-maid kitty:
Oh, what a hard life!

*Practical consequences of "Objective truth as non-existent or unknowable": The best we can do is approach consensus, harmony with respect, care, and tolerance for others' take on reality. If we can't establish absolute truth, but merely approximations, it follows we can't establish absolute good or bad. Hence no one is inherently right or wrong. This is not to say there isn't a great deal to be learned from human expression and behavior within the realm of the bulk of human experience, more toward the center, between the polar extremes where most of us dwell. Through the ages we've shown that we can and do accept certain representations of the truth as part of the core narrative—until popular opinion shifts and a new truth/fact/reality gets articulated, popularized, and finally supplants the pre-existing manifestation.

One of the nasty little truths, right under our noses but not exactly heralded in public discussions, concerns America's sacred document, the Constitution. For such progressive ideals as stated in Jefferson's Declaration of Independence, citizenship in our newly-formed Union was limited to property-owning white males. No women were included in citizenship—not enfranchised until 1920(?). African Americans were chattel, value was set as 5/8 of a Caucasian for taxation purposes and not even proportional voting rights, Native Americans (*What, the savages?*), or non-property owning adults considered; none had the full rights of citizenship.

Thus, the transitory nature of our core "truths."

*If one perceives oneself as unloved beyond a certain point, the perception changes to being *unlovable*, a *terra incognito* of great suffering …

Time is a construct on which to hang observed events sequentially. For a long time I contemplated the appropriateness of the word *observed* in the forgoing statement. I've come to think it is appropriate and necessary. Clearly uncountable events occur outside our awareness and, hence, go unobserved. But does the concept of Time pertain to those unaccounted/able events? I think not. Time, be it geologic time, or astronomic "time," is simply a metric we *Homo sapiens* employ to measure such intervals/sequences.

*<u>To pair or not to pair</u>

(with a bow to ee cummings)
maybe you
may us be:
i be May

*The flickering candle slowly consumed itself down its tapered stem while the icicles out my window yielded their cold, rigid daggers to the hint of warmth. I let my attention dissipate, lose its sharp focus, atomize into the perimeter of my perceptions. No more distinction between *this* and *that*, no more *A* and *not A*, no dualities, a surrender of cause and effect. Swathed in my blanket, warm and content from a full day with nothing, not even guilt from such self-indulgence and sloth, to disturb my suspended consciousness, it was an absence of sensation, of recognition of *self*.

Yet after an indeterminate time, with the candle guttering its faltering light, I was aroused back to my sense of location and being. The eternal verities remained; gravity and the time continuum/ compendium were restored. Nothing lasts forever and it was time to reengage my place in the busy context of existence.

*Rights? I decline to talk about rights unless we include responsibilities in the same breath.

Coming of age: What is that, arriving at some level of maturity? Unless it's an arbitrary chronological standard, how would we know? I propose that the term represent the age by which one assumes the privileges—and responsibilities—of a citizen, an emancipated adult. If the above observation is applicable to the individual, might it also work metaphorically in terms of our social structures, our nation-states and communities? Thereby raising the question, How and When might we, collectively, "come of age?"

At the individual level, the notion applies to one's privileges/responsibilities in relation to fellow humans. A person unwilling or unable to assume those responsibilities should not be fully emancipated, and thus, remain a ward of the state in one capacity or another. At the collective level, Coming of Age needs to apply not only to the human community but the biosphere, as well. Communities that refuse to act responsibly toward other human communities *or* biologic niches should be sanctioned.

*Big Bang

All,
of a sudden
impulse, born?

*Post Eden: Rules are conceived and implemented (only?) in the absence of a willingness of people to act responsibly, i.e., on behalf of *Community first, self, second.*

*I toss this ripe, red apple before you
if you love me truly
take it and invite me to your arms
but if, alas, you will not
keep the apple anyway and ponder
how long its freshness and beauty last.

*<u>Ponderous ephemerae</u>

smoke & mirrors
shadows & lies
brief encounters
long goodbyes

*I think perhaps
the most profound insight
I've become aware of
is the notion of the Time Continuum/
Compendium: the idea that no matter
how insignificant the attempt in life
nothing is ever lost
nothing is forever but everything
is linked   has an effect

                a consequence

Prostrate in advancing twilight

Prostrate in advancing twilight
Beethoven violin concerto
infuses my audible environment
having just lit the peace pipe
watching a hapless cockroach
the size of your big toe
writhe and squirm—partially
crushed by an inert insecticide
spray can wielded by unseen hand
reluctant to mash its cream cheese
entrails onto already grimy floor
I think to render the death throes
tame by exhaling in its direction
ambrosial effluvia slowly wreathe
a toxic cloud—poor smashed demon
responds by racing three upended legs
wildly but uselessly in the air
now in agony or fatigue the pace
is slowed but the dancing tarantella
of strings pours on unabated
oblivious to this creature death

(Athens, 1965)

On being a barbarian

Have you ever had the experience of suddenly seeing yourself as others see you? On Halloween some years ago in Japan, my wife got lured into helping her Japanese associate at an English institute host a party for 60-some children. I was implored to come also, time permitting, as only one other native speaker had been corralled into participating. As some kind of luck would have it, I was free that afternoon and so followed along out of curiosity.

The associate had gone to no little effort in organizing the "Halloween Experience," at least as she perceived it. In a lesser-used classroom she had placed tables down the center of the room. On the table near the entrance, a series of black vinyl bags were arranged, their openings snugged with rubber bands. The first bag contained peeled grapes suggesting—you guessed it—eyeballs! The second held cold, gelatinous spaghetti noodles, evocative to the fervid imagination of entrails; finely chopped tomatoes, resembling somebody's notion of mashed brains, festered in the third bag.

The other *gaijin* was decked out in a ghoulish mask and I in iridescent fright wig. We were to foster the understanding that the assorted body parts were gleaned from hapless sheep, but we might as well have claimed viscera from human origin since essentially no one believed—let alone *understood*—us anyway. When you ask a kid to stick his hand into a bag to determine its contents, he's likely to haul out a fistful for closer inspection, which happened more often than not. After weathering the creepy-feely experience the kids, allowed into the room in groups of four, were coaxed down the table for apple bobbing. Reward? The bobbed apple and a small bag of candy. Occasionally, curious mothers asked to observe the proceedings from positions in the background. Dozens of blown-up balloons littered the floor, though it was difficult to say to what effect.

The chamber was, of course, darkened to heighten the aural and tactile effect. I crouched behind a table conjuring up "unearthly" sounds by rubbing a finger across a balloon surface, and uttered grunts and guttural moans as the other gaijin yanked open the door and snatched the next set of kids—much to the shock, dismay, and occasional amusement of many, especially the boys.

Alas, however, among some of the younger girls, the whole phantasmagoria was more than their innocent, fun-loving minds could handle. Let's face it, we gaijin, even in standard trappings, are beyond the ken of some of these folks; what do you expect when we get freaked up and try to spook a bunch of seven-year olds? They are apt to wax hysterical and need a little consoling by the likes of my wife and other "normal" folks in the vicinity.

It was in such a moment, midst the shrieks and gales of tears, that I happened to glance at a couple of housewives along the wall, mouths slightly agape, staring at this scene in utter disbelief. I had this sensation of instant prescience; I felt I could read their minds.

They were thinking, what a strange and unfathomable culture these people come from that they make a holiday "celebrating" ghosts, monsters, witches, and other such fearful specters in order to scare the pee out of little girls...

(Kugenuma Kaigan, Japan, Halloween 1994)

Fugue in *Bu* major

The following was inspired by a sustained, 28-second solo on my own personal wind instrument, in the shower after a hearty evening—scant hours after a splendid repast. A true, multi-sensory event it was: not only aurally noteworthy but olfactorily, as well. Said instrument has the virtue of being anatomical, thus not needing to be lugged around and separately mislaid, broken, or lost. Affording many effectively spontaneous opportunities to practice one's *art*. It requires great effort and concentration to produce much in the way of tonal variation; I have thus far mastered only a low staccato roar with minimal modulation. Doubtless many months, if not years, of diligent practice will be required, as in any great artistic expression, before a level of success is forthcoming.

One envisions a marching band of indeterminate number. Adequately trained, perhaps as few as 10 or 12 would suffice. Snappily dressed in matching uniforms, stepping off in perfect unison—can't you just see them? Brass-buttoned, sky-blue outfits complete with the "Queen Nefertiti" beaver band hats with leather chin straps, and shiny black boots. The uniforms would be cut away for the *instruments* to appear unfettered, and not unduly muffle the clarion report. Painted a bright yellow, I should think, to call visual attention to the source of such heraldic blasts.

At strategic intervals along the parade route including, certainly, before the visiting dignitaries and judging stands, the

Band Major/Majorette would signal the musicians and, without missing a step and with scarcely more than a stiffening of the facial muscles (as noted by the most astute observers), a sort of "barked" version of *Yankee Doodle* might issue forth, to the astonishment of one and all. Stunned, more than a few people would be "moved to tears" while others reflexively reach for handkerchiefs or towels, trying to stifle the wave of uncontrolled hacking and watery eyes that seems to accompany the spectacle. With experimentation, performance-day diets could be individually tailored to achieve maximum metabolic effect.

If these proud band members were to have a group name, something suggestive of a distinctive floral fragrance would be entirely suitable. Perhaps, the *Gamboling Gardenias*? Or the *Sauntering Sub-Rosas?*

(June 2003)

Approaching homeostasis,
the "perfect world"

The perfect world for a writer would entail frequent visitations by the muse. Not mere visitations, either. The source of inspiration would have to pretty much occupy the psyche of the person involved (if not the loins, as well) so that, in thrall of the creative event, the identity of the muse and the mortal vessel become indistinguishable and, albeit fleetingly, inseparable. This artist in acting out his/her art, in channeling the muse, becomes the vehicle for the expression, while, no doubt, the act of creation takes on the style of the artist. The perfect world, being subjective, would require a different interpretation for each person, many of them in conflict with each other.

So why care we about the *perfect* world? There doesn't seem to be evidence of sustained "perfection" in any aspect of social interaction, currently or historically. In moments of reflection we readily concede that we humans are far from prefect. Given that we accept—or at least accommodate—our individual imperfections, it follows that our collective efforts would be flawed too. Lo and behold, a casual overview of history confirms blatant and continuous imperfection, at minimum, in the various expressions of ethnocentrism. Mark that 5,000 years of *Us vs. Them.*

So isn't it a vanity to preoccupy oneself with idle notions of an unachievable perfect world? If we know with a high degree of certainty that the world will not be made perfect, with or without our efforts, in any of our lifetimes (and a credible line of thinking would say, *No perfection, ever*), then why not occupy one's attention with more plausible, realistic campaigns? Why not, indeed!

The question, simply posed: Of what possible use could a construct (such as *perfection*) be, if it has no analog in the real world, nothing to actually measure it by? And to repeat, regarding the realm of human relationships, it may be illogical to expect any manifestation of perfection.

First off, I'll assert that even if perfection is an abstraction with no literal human counterpart, it still has validity in that it serves as a direction by which progress, or failure, may be marked. We haven't yet established an even roughed-out notion of perfection and even if we were able to come up with such a construct, it's unlikely we'll have anything like universal acceptance.

Garden of Eden? Heaven on Earth? What could possibly be "perfection" for so many different people from so many different lands and cultures? It's probably going to have to be a pretty broad-stroke outline in order to allow various peoples an interpretation that fits their particular needs. Surely one articulation could take the long view on optimizing potential for survivability by achieving homeostasis, balance, and sustainability with the rest of the biosphere. A social matrix would be far shy of perfect if it were conditioned on heavy over-consumption of resources to sustain its "prosperity," or "success."

Beyond biospheric homeostasis, the notion of perfection, in the social context (utopia?), would need to be interpreted and continuously reinterpreted by the participants, the stake-holders in the outcome.

The Carnage of War

The battle had been waged; it was all over
in a few desperate, cacophonous hours.
The purple-crested warriors had grown
complacent in their five-month primacy,
their growing potency and numbers.
They lay lifeless now, still bodies
strewn helter-skelter 'midst the verdant summer
field. Some composed as if sleeping,
many more mangled, hacked into pieces
in random groupings, here and there
slaughtered singletons. No more
roar of battle, no lingering screams.
Only utter stillness over the whole
of the battlefield where not one
proud warrior longer stood.

(In memoriam to a battalion of Foxglove
who lost their lives/succumbed to a field mower
in an Oregon Coast Range meadow

June 2005)

Doing good by doing well

How are you doing?

Doin' good, You?

Every time I hear this or somesuch variation, I experience an involuntary twitch; I have to bite my tongue, preventing me from unloading my well-rehearsed lecture on the "Difference between Adjectives and Adverbs." All together now: Adjectives modify, clarify, and otherwise tell us about nouns. Adverbs, when they aren't busy modifying adjectives, usually modify, clarify, and tell us about verbs. True, *good* can be a stand-alone pronoun, as in the Three Virtues of Socrates: the good, the true, and the beautiful (meaning *life,* one surmises). For the most part, however, it is an adjective. Note the nouns it modifies in the following examples:

Good dog, fetch the stick!

Good Heavens, they're here early!

The food in that restaurant is good, but expensive.

Ergo, in the opening conversation, the respondent should have said something to the effect, *I'm doing <u>well</u>, thank you. And you?*

No, I'm not acting as the self-appointed Grammar Police and, yes, languages change all the time, though I admit resisting this particular change on the grounds that it *de*clarifies and obfuscates communication. It may be that the interlocutors are willing to accept a higher level of ambiguity in their interaction, but I take it as given that communication is usually an imprecise-enough negotiation of meaning without deliberately adding to the challenge. To me, the more accurately and precisely we are able to articulate our requests, impressions, and opinions, the more likely we are able to accurately share the human experience (*social* animals that we are). And the intentional vagueness and ambiguity can get relegated to connoting a poetic or otherwise artistic experience, where the independence of interpretation is not only acceptable but perhaps desirable. At the opposite extreme, perhaps formulaic greetings qualify, also.

There is, however, an interesting exception to this general rule in the semantic/syntactic uses of *good*, and it is for this reason that I've dragged you through this rather tedious exercise in didactic pedantry. It is, of course, possible to do good deeds and be recognized for same in one's lifetime. Some of our exemplars of right conduct, those who sacrificed aspects of their lives for the good of others (Mother Theresa and Nelson Mandela leap to mind), are rightfully thought of as good people because of the beneficial results of their conduct. But the great dilemma, the Catch 22, is that these people are not permitted—bordering on taboo—to ascribe the goodness of their acts *unto themselves.*

If one truly does good work in the world, it is absolutely necessary that others be the source of such recognition. Thus we have the odd situation of someone acknowledging doing well and in so saying, may have coincidentally done good—there's simply no way to know, *a priori.* However, in the instance of one who claims to doing good, we can safely conclude that s/he has *not* done good since, by convention, the attribution may come only from external sources. Said person, by claiming to do good, may, in fact, be doing well—except in botched word choice/usage.

(April 2006)

A funny story

The ancient Greeks were like most other groups throughout history: Protective, in-grown, and suspicious of outsiders. In a word, ethnocentric. People outside one's ethnic community were barbarians (*varvaroi*). During my first sojourn to modern *Ellas* (1961), tourism was a relatively new phenomenon, with the exception of Athens and possibly the Cyclades isle of Mykonos. But tourists are sometimes a subtle and corrupting—or is it corrupt*ed*?—influence on the general trend of things.

It was usually novel enough to pass merely as a *xenos*, or foreigner, during my earlier stay, but these days bring different types of strangers, more exotic ways to flaunt one's ethnicity. For the average Greek, it is seemingly important to differentiate among the *xenoi* by testing one's intuition in guessing the nationality. I am often taken for a German (*Germanos*), and fair complexion, straggly beard, and "autostop" as my chief mode of transportation naturally make this a fair guess, especially since Germans make up the majority of tourists these days. My standard ploy is to answer, No, I'm Greek!—inevitably drawing an initial pause of shock, then disbelief.

Of course, the most provincial dolt or churl could see that I'm anything but a native; still, in a way this piques their curiosity and renews the effort. I often encourage their dilemma by accusing them of not believing me. When they freely admit they don't, I ask if it matters where I'm from? This is a mini-*coup* to most; they agree unwillingly that where one is from is not a core question, especially upon engaging a conversation with this *other*, thereby making it personal. Nonetheless, my claim of "Greekness" is not altogether untrue: Having lived in Greece now a year and a half, there is much of the Greek in me; I adapted quite well. I am apt to say I am *Ellinas sto cardia,* or Greek at heart.

On the approach to Larissa by bus this evening, the passengers and driver became involved in the standard inquiry when you've got a conspicuous in-group/out-group situation— guessing the foreigner's identity. Finally, the driver bade me occupy the elevated copilot seat opposite him for better scrutiny. While still not knowing my nationality, this same bus driver offered me his 20-year-old sister's hand in marriage!

I was stunned, thinking, you've no idea how incongruous and bizarre this is, having been on the road since 7:30 this morning fleeing Athens and, somewhat bruised and broken, a Greek/ American liaison. Maintaining the conversation, I asked about the *prika* (dowry). He assured me there was a pastry shop and a clothing store from which I could choose…

As if on cue, the Larissa central square bus stop, my destination for the day, hove into view. In the commotion of off-loading passengers and goods, the question was left unresolved, it should be noted, with both notions of dignity intact.

(Spring 1966)

Spontaneous anarchy: a walk in the park

Easter Sunday this year was distinguished by the resurrection of pleasant weather. We denizens of the Pacific Northwest are used to sharing this holiday with variations of inclement weather: storms, drizzle, day-on-week-on-month overcast, deluge, wind, and approximately as much chance of snow as pure, unadulterated sun. So while we didn't quite achieve that mythic sunny condition, we did experience the day without any precipitation: good for the kiddies in their Easter egg hunts, and the shuttling to and from sites of ritualistic psychic mollification—but also quite fortuitous for the other occasion of celebration: Four-Twenty!

On the off chance that there are still folks out there yet unfamiliar with the Four-Twenty phenomenon, allow me to guide you through the intricacies. Origins remain a little vague, but most credible vectors seem to lead back to Marin County in the early 1970s. As the San Francisco "flower children" scene gave way to Haight-Ashbury moochers and free loaders in the late 1960s, the Grateful Dead and entourage relocated north across the Golden Gate Bridge, causing ripples in the local community still felt to this day. Then as now high school malcontents of the newly testosterone-challenged variety were prone to non-compliance with the onerous rules and regulations that make up the rites of passage from marginally functional hominids to tractable, obedient, wage scrabbling, and tax paying citizens. Such students were and are readily identified, and the more

301

egregious among them detained after the normal schedule of lessons for further indoctrination into society's expectations. Thus, around 1971 or '2 a counterculture seed was germinated, a code developed, a shorthand signal at a San Rafael high school, that swift rescue from detention would be waiting in the form of miscreant comrades in an escape vehicle from a designated spot in front of the school upon the release of the malefactors. Promptly at 4:20 pm, these juvenile delinquents were to be whisked away to a prearranged, secluded area not far from town where they were to be rewarded for the indignities they suffered at school.

What manner of reward, you ask? Nothing less than that scourge of Western Civilization, marijuana, *aka* reefer, boo, grass, weed, pot, ganja, dope, the viper, and so on—that first modest step before hurtling into the hopeless Abyss where degradation and defilement await. The horror! Four-Twenty slowly morphed into a signal for the opportunity to partake in the noble herb. Ultimately, however, it is far less important how the event happened, than that it happened.

The first time I noticed the phenomenon came as a bit of a shock because I hadn't yet associated the date with marijuana ingestion. On previous years on April 20th when weather permitted, I was apt to take walks in my neighborhood Mt. Tabor Park. About five years ago, by chance, I encountered a few groups engaged in celebrating the occasion at the park summit; thus, my introduction. On this particular occasion I was ready, anticipatory even. Thor and Zeus had collaborated by withholding the normal ravages of the season, and the Christian deity complied by giving us the spring rite of Easter simultaneously. Auspicious! Or not.

The top of Mt. Tabor sports an oval no-vehicle roadway, which loops from the south end around the East side down to a small parking area, connecting drivable roads to picnic areas, kiddie playgrounds, and so on. Inside the oval on the south end looms the bronze statue of Harvey W. Scott, a Portland stalwart of a century ago, cast by Gutzon Borglum of Mt. Rushmore fame. Among the encomia chiseled in the base of the statue, in addition to Publisher and Editor of the Oregonian, is Molder of Opinion. Harve was younger brother to Abagail Scott Dunniway, Oregon's preeminent suffragette, and one of the nation's most outspoken and articulate advocates for women's enfranchisement. Little brother, this small-minded big shot, was in an ideal position to support big sister in her decades-long campaign. Instead, ol' *molder-of-opinion* Harve hedged, resisted, and equivocated the emancipation of women. What a guy!

At the north end and the literal peak of the hill stands the Wicca Tree, a gnarled and twisted Broadleaf Maple of beauty and age, a photogenic background to any number of weddings, receptions and other rituals throughout the year. Most of the mature evergreens in the vicinity are Doug Fir, with open spaces maintained for picnicking and views of Mt. Hood and the downtown area. A dazzling Sakura, or flowering cherry, was in full bloom in the middle of the oval. I made a complete pass around the loop to take stock of the scene: perhaps 150~180 people, strolling on the roadway, seated on the damp ground in groups of a few to 30 or so, lots of singles and couples, a few babies/kids with family members. I settled into a perch on a slope above the roadway with a view of the city to the west, and enjoyed a ringside seat of the ensuing parade. When a spectacular display of imaginative self-adornment passed before me, some combination of dazzle and prance, I applauded loudly and thanked them for their performance. Across from me, the *de rigueur* drum presence occupied a couple of park benches: a conga played by a spastic practitioner, and a bongo set manned by Two Feather Timmy, a wizened Native American who called out at every pause in the thumping, "Who's got a beer?" It was clear he was not in desperate need.

One would be inclined to think the greeting on such a day would be "Happy Easter!" and, indeed, it was heard, especially in the early afternoon, by park patrons unaware of the day's other celebration. As the afternoon progressed, however, the interactive salute graduated to "Hi!", though we'd be referring to the homonym, "High," as startled Easter celebrants gave way to increasing numbers of stoners of various description.

There were chameleons of all ages, those people who, in appearance and persona, would pass for straight; and aging veterans like myself, the elders, no longer willing to disguise our association with the fringe of society. But the large majority of the attendees were young folks—teens to mid-thirties—who turned out in droves, many in wild costumes both Easter bunny, as well as "Alice in Wonderland," inspired. One young man clearly pleased with himself was clad in a full body Tigger suit befitting nothing so much as a light-hearted occasion with like-minded folks. A girl pranced about costumed as Tinker Bell, delighting and delighted by the day, enjoying herself. But the day was special for its array of Easter "bonnets:" There were bowlers and fedoras, cowboy hats of the Stevie Ray Vaughn variety (straightforward hat festooned with a gaudy, trailing hat band, and feathers), and top hats of every bizarre freak style, and hue in the rainbow.

People made eye contact with wide grins. There was a sense of in group/out group identity distinctions based on this one shared experience, reinforced by the realization that here in Oregon simple possession of this benign plant is still illegal. Our act of defiance had potentially serious consequences…if the state felt compelled to utilize valuable jurisprudence resources and treasury to pursue it. Which it doesn't, as we proved that day. Still, there was a kind of giddy feeling, as the joints and the pipes and bongs were passed around. Plus-or-minus 250 people (adjusting for the early leavers and the late comers) engaged in a collective nose thumbing of this law.

Note to politicians, lawmakers and social architects of any stripe: Attitudes are always in flux. When a law falls out of favor by such a significant portion of society that people openly flaunt it, it would be wise to abolish said law summarily lest the populous lose faith in *all* laws, *all* lawmakers, and law enforcers.

One could sense as the day progressed that some ineffable expectation was building. With 4:20 pm approaching there was a feeling that, what, we would all be transformed into a righteous cadre for Peace, Love, and Harmony? A progressive group galvanized into a campaign for social justice? Or a drooling horde of Welfare sponges who breed like rabbits? Nobody I talked to had any clear sense. But as the time drew nigh, many celebrants gathered toward the center of the oval with calls to "Make a circle!" Some 2/3 or ¾ of us complied, thinking, I suppose, this was a good, touchy-feely way to demonstrate somesort of solidarity. However, the remainder—groups, couples, and singletons here and there—decided to exercise their right to remain aloof from any type of central "planning." Anarchy, at its most basic level.

Lacking polish

Lacking Polish polish
a patchy Apache
discussed disgust
in poached petulance

Noise of news
a minute minuet
the second second
where matter matters
these theses
thwarted thought

Support our troops: a deconstruction

If one were on or near a city street for any length of time ca 2005, one could not avoid noticing, owing to their ubiquity, a thin piece of flexible, magnetized material made to look like a loop of ribbon, often yellow but sometimes redwhiteandblue, attached to the trunk of a car. They become easily visible from quite a distance, especially after you've seen them a few times. You need to be pretty close to read the script on the loop, however. Invariably, it says *Support our troops*. What follows is my interpretation of this text through an exploration of definitions and assumptions.

Troops, a plural noun, are the uniformed personnel of a nation's military. I take it as self-evident that organized societies operate, at least ostensibly, by the rule of law. A legal system implies law enforcement, since no society yet has achieved 100% compliance with all its laws. While it is wise to try to enact laws that benefit the greatest number of people most of the time, and cultivate the best environment for law abiding, we have not yet been able to prevent some of the citizenry from socially damaging behavior. If police are our domestic law enforcers, then by extension, the military becomes our international law/treaty enforcer.

Our, a possessive adjective, is a deictic term calling attention to the following noun's ownership. In deixis, a dichotomy exists: *this* implies a *that; here* implies a *there.*

Something that is *ours* is not possessed by everyone. Whatever group we are members of, the distinction of *we/us* (inferred and necessary to complete the meaning of *our*) sets *us* up as being different from *them*. The troops are not other people's; they are ours. Troops belonging to other people are not (as) worthy of our support. Or so this simplistic imperative seems to imply. Well, right off the implied assumptions are suspect.

The notion that Iraq was somehow a threat to the USA, an *us vs. them* characterization, is a false dichotomy. There's very little, if any, of my identity (*me* in the *we/us*) that makes up the America that chooses to invade a sovereign nation, no matter how odious its autocrat, no matter how needful the oil. Has the rule of international law devolved into "The strong get to decide *who* the bad guys are, *what* the course of action is, and *when* and *where* this takes place"? The answer seems to be Yes, the strong *do* decide (international law be damned!) but they do not act on my behalf.

Needless to say, *them* in the equation, *us vs. them*, is also suspect. The notion of the familiar configuration of Iraq (or any other nation, for that matter) as sacrosanct is folly. If it were to splinter into three or more geographic divisions, each more homogeneous and stable than the awkward and untenable old Iraq, then so be it.

Support, as a verb, is more problematic. To the extent our social order needs protection from international threats of a traditional military nature, I willingly support our troops. Which is to say, I acknowledge they act on my behalf; I accept that portion of my taxes that applies to our military in that instance. But, aside from this rather limited range of support, I find myself mostly disagreeing/disapproving of the deployment and application of America's armed forces. Thus, because I haven't found a way to exempt my taxation from America's military (larger than the next 18 countries, in descending expenditures, of the rest of the world's military *combined!*), I support the troops financially, with objection. Especially, when they are engaged in actions other than strictly providing protection from international threats—decidedly *not* the case with Iraq. Beyond taxes, I feel no compunction to demonstrate support for America's military, certainly not the affective mode of support that one might display in, say, booster loyalty for the "home team" (e.g., waving banners, wearing T-shirts, ball caps, spouting patriotic jingoes).

Otherwise, beyond taxation, I'm frankly at a loss as to how one might "support our troops." This seems to me to be an insidious form of chauvinism, a means to insure citizens' unexamined support. Our military presence in Iraq is such an unalloyed tragedy that I find this booster syndrome grotesque. It is a tragedy because American military personnel and support have allowed themselves to be placed in a kill-or-be-killed situation for specious reasons. Thus they kill, and are killed, while the tragedy grinds on. But we are all complicit, are we not? Collectively, we consent to this colossal tragedy. We all have blood on our hands.

Having considered the content of the message, the final element I need to address is the message form. There is an implied subject (*you*) and the statement takes the form of an injunction, a command. The bearer of this message is not asking you; s/he is ordering you to support our troops. Which instantly raises the counter-question, *Or what?* What do you have in mind if I/we don't "support our troops," say, in the occupation of Iraq? An all-expenses-paid (courtesy of our government), extended vacation in Gitmo, incommunicado, as a suspected terrorist sympathizer?

Support our troops is a cheap sentiment with essentially no meaning. Weasel words, nothing more.

(Fall 2005)

In the dark

Some things are better
in the dark:
Tactile, sensual connectivity,
touch of electric skin
doesn't need light, is only distracted,
diminished by illumination.

With music,
the aural sweep
of melody and rhythm
become evocative, arousing the shadows,
stirring unbidden feelings.
Light adds little.

As in sensuality and music,
sometimes words only
get in the way.

(February 2006)

Aesthetic parameters

"When it comes to aesthetics," she said, "anything from simple balance and harmony to spectacular complexity and intricacy, you've got your 'man-made,' and you've got your 'created by God.' Of course, man-made is really God-made one step removed, if you know what I mean."

Uneasily, "I guess if you permit enough leeway as to the definition and meaning of *God* and *create/make*, I'll go along. And the dichotomy of types or origins of beauty makes sense to me, depending on the context. But if you are imagining an extrinsic, monotheistic, Abrahamic (Judeo-Christian-Muslim) deity who out of Nothing commanded into existence the universe and, more importantly to us, Earth teeming with life, hence the creator of beauty... well, if such is your orientation, I profoundly disagree," he said, and quickly heaved a couple of deep breaths.

After a tense pause, she sputtered, "Well, that's just blasphemy. How can you turn your back on your community, your country, your heritage? Besides, who else could create the heavens and the earth? I simply can't believe you, and shouldn't even be talking to you. That attitude will assure you a quick trip to hell!"

"If such a place exists, and if we really do possess discrete, 'immortal' souls to be sanctified or damned, no doubt I'll take up some sort of residence there. But I'll be in very good company! Believe me or not, it's your prerogative, but you ought to hear me out. It won't hurt you to examine another point of view. To me, the complexity and variety, the marvel and mystery, and yes, the exquisite beauty of life, is miraculous enough without needing a Supreme Being, or creation myth." More relaxed now, in the zone, "Such a creature may have been useful in the nascent days of human civilization; today it is an ill-fitting metaphor, little more than a vestigial appendage, a superfluity, of interest to paleo-anthropologists, ethnologists, theologists and their ilk, otherwise a hindrance, an obstacle.

"Incidentally, while I have deep admiration and respect for the artists of any culture or age, any artistic expression, I've become conscious of my significant preference for the *natural* sources of beauty, not for 'worship,' per se, but certainly reverence-worthy. I appreciate and expand my wonder every time I immerse myself in the *non*-human-made world. The popularity of the Grand Canyon, Yellowstone and Yosemite, among other wonders, attest to our collective awe of spectacular natural places. Additionally, many of us have our more private, special places where we can, as the Japanese might say, 'forest bathe'— walk slowly, quietly, or better yet sit quietly, surrounded visually and aurally by a natural setting. Beauty, and its recognition and appreciation in any form, surely enriches us, and makes life worthwhile."

Sadhana

Seeking spiritual guidance
I came upon a monastery
where a noted guru resided.
I asked the gate attendant,
Is this a yoga monastery?
The man smiled faintly
and asked in return,
Does it matter, friend?
I said I'm a little afraid
of yoga. I've seen some
of the exercises. My bones are
brittle, my joints stiff. I'm
afraid you'd expect too much
of me. With that same slight smile
he replied, it would be only
what you expect of yourself.

(Amritsar, Punjab, India 1966)

No help from heaven

Heaven, assuming somesuch entity exists, is purported to be many things; a place where the souls of virtuous Christians reside throughout eternity without strife; where only peace, love, and harmony prevail. It's left pretty vague. No one on this side of the divide actually knows exactly *how* one passes through eternity in peace, love and harmony. More to the point, in what manifestation of soul, what vessel would we inhabit, in order to appreciate eternity in terms we, the living, might understand. Still, there is one compelling realization we can take away from an analysis of what we *do* know about heaven, and life on earth.

As a reward for a life of obedience to God, and perhaps some other factors—virtuous conduct, servant of one's fellow human, etc.—depending on the particular sect within the vast umbrella of the Christian faith one adheres to, one is led to believe that one is entitled to an idyllic eternity, when one departs this mortal coil. That may be true, and for all you True Believers, I certainly hope you receive the heaven you deserve. However, in terms of direct, empirical connection of people living here on earth to occupants of heaven, its administration, maintenance, or any other agency associated with the concept of heaven, we'd have to say there is none. No interaction.

Heaven may, indeed, be a great way to wile away eternity, but in terms of life continuing down here on earth, heaven is passive and mute. So the message I draw is, if you have any concern for life on earth, in any particular expression you'd care to make pertaining to the way things are, or ought to be, you'd better get to it. Attend to matters you care about here and now. Nothing lasts. Get going, because soon enough, the beings we think of as "you" and "me" will perhaps exist as a memory among others only—and for a short while, at that.

Whereas the already-deceased occupants of heaven, again, assuming somesort of conscious entity transcends life on earth, will be reduced to mere observers of worldly affairs. Only we, among the still-kicking, can act out as a part of the individual human, family, and/or community drama. Being alive entitles us to our own role. After we're "gone" the best we can hope for, if the Christians have it right, is to *watch* the performance here on *terra firma*; mere spectators from Paradise, nothing more. Ugh!

It (all) is

To my friends:
part of me cherishes you
part of me despises you
part of me barely knows you

To my foes:
part of me despises you
part of me cherishes you
part of me recognizes you too well

It's the same me
being you and me
and being caught
by the space between
and the conjoining

Intoxication

An argument can be made that the dreary, repetitive nature of life is the inspiration and driver of intoxication—our fascination with "drugs." Since we are mortal, we are eminently fallible. If I were a believer in the divine, I'd say God asks a lot of us to endure the numbing tedium of the routine. Except that He-She-It also provides the means of the "vacation." The losing of oneself in the connection with all else. Or seeing the miraculous interconnected-ness of all being with "new" eyes, the I-Thou.

To sustain the unrelenting slog of the treadmill over the long haul appears to be all but unendurable, beyond human capability, without occasional flights of otherness. The business of living is simply intolerable without breaks, opportunities for escape, the ability to get out of oneself for a while. Humanity's intoxicants throughout the millennia have provided exactly that respite from the harsh glare of being that which is expected by others. Since intoxicants are so universal cross-culturally, throughout history, it is clear they serve a social function, though often sanctioned, as per the Saturnalias, Lupercalias, Bacchanalias, Carnivals, and other assorted toots. Intoxicants represent a socially recognized, if not approved, way to step outside one's social self, one's familiar set of responsibilities and obligations, for a respite.

Logically, I suppose, one should aspire to the "golden mean," that area between the consistent, predictable, and plodding repetitiveness of dubious virtue, versus the loose, flexible, and risky let-it-all-hang-out in our roles and identities. That middle ground would doubtless be more desirable than taking either extreme too seriously: the soulless automaton drudge vs. the floater, the butterfly flitting from one to another blossom of excitement and opportunity.

Thus, the lure of copping a buzz, getting out of one's head, imbibing the forbidden fruits of the gods. The difficulty lies in the tendency of us humans to over-indulge our intoxicants, when given the chance. *If a little is good, more is better* is patently untrue, and we know from experience that it is not true. Everything in life has limits. But, hey, it's a holiday! What's a holiday for, if not to get a little loose with friends? Like moths to the flame, we are inexorably drawn to that blazing light of Now Possibilities.

Forgiveness

Forgiveness is an unresolved issue for me, I'm a little ashamed to say. You'd think a man of my age... At an intellectual level, perhaps even a moral level, I understand and accept the reasoning for forgiving the slings and arrows of one's adversaries. My over-arching difficulty, however, is offering forgiveness—i.e., faith and trust fully restored; suspension of ill will, thoughts of revenge—without some indication of regret or contrition from the source of the wound in question.

I can be charitable. I *want* to be charitable and forgiving. What is that old saw? *To err is human, to forgive, divine.* A swell sentiment, to be sure. But if a person appears to bear me a grudge, it doesn't seem wise for me to rely on forgiveness for previous acts of hostility as my first response, especially if he continues to indicate he bears me ill will. For me, a little vigilance and caution precede outright forgiveness. Is that being overly defensive? Setting too cautious a standard? I think I demonstrate contrition for my mistakes, show sincere regret for my blunders (both of them... *Ha!*). Is it unreasonable to want that reciprocated? Renewed trust can be earned, and with it will come forgiveness. Meanwhile, it may be a trifle rash to expect it to appear soon, or all at once. Especially, from such a battle-scarred old cynic as me.

Everybody screws up. We're finite, frequently fallible fools—human, in short. Of course we err. Whether we are conscious of it or not, we impose upon untold numbers of others, humans and other life forms, and thus at some level, entreat forgiveness for our transgressions. So it absolutely behooves us to reciprocate in fully absolving the slights, barbs, and abrasions perceived to have been inflicted on us. Still, a part of me says, *Yep, just as soon as the scoundrels manifest a glint of humility.* I wonder if I am unique in this regard. I hope not.

A Buddhist might say, there's a good deal too much "you" in all that presumption of defining "justice" and meting it out. It's an anchor on your ability to have a higher, more inclusive consciousness, inasmuch as a part of your brain is devoted to getting back at this or that person who dared to treat you with ill-respect. Humility starts with you. One could argue, your inflated and somewhat calcified ego needs the shakeup of having someone taunt you, make fun of your lifestyle, your quaint ideas, just to keep in check that ol' high-and-mighty tendency. If you take yourself too seriously, you are just asking for a fall. Or so a *Bo-san*, a Buddhist priest, might say. Don't forget that a bellicose redneck asshole all in your face... is just another test to see what it will take to blow your cool. You *win* by not degenerating into a spoiled-child tantrum, on account of life not going the way you want it to.

It is rather easy to recognize the righteous, logical and moral bases for forgiving—and being forgiven—from the comfort of your own study in a moment of relaxed contemplation. In the throes of the argument, however, a survival mechanism seems to kick in automatically, and my responses and calculations become far more defensive than might have been the case a few minutes before. Not sure I see the connection, thus a non sequitur alert!, but this apparent resistance to forgive others suggests a lingering insecurity/over-protectiveness of self, or significant doubts of self-worth, based on a couple of assumptions.

1) The people most comfortable with who they are, flaws and all, in front of other people (politicians, preachers, and other

snake oil purveyors) are the ones least likely to get ruffled by the average public heckler. Hazards of the trade.

2) The people least comfortable with who they are, particularly in public settings, are most apt to be sensitive to criticism, even when it amounts to nothing more than a point of view. Worth nothing unless you, the recipient, decide to pursue it.

This would be a good time to show forgiveness. Not so much absolution of those "guilty" parties, but forgiveness in order to secure one's own release. Like many another facet of human experience, it may be that one learns forgiveness—*if* one learns forgiveness—case by case, one small step at a time.

Let us give thanks

Let us give thanks
for the many benefits we enjoy:
for sun and moon, stars and earth;
for the Locus that gives us life, then rhythm,
then beauty: valleys, rain, forests, rivers,
mountains, lakes, meadows and seas.
And for the sanctuary of a back yard.

Let us give thanks for life,
the connections of life on which we depend:
our loved ones, family, and friends. All the lives
that depend on us—the nasty little microbial colony
growing under my toenails. The queendom
of carpenter ants living in my walls. The rats
taking up residence in my compost pile.
My cranky old-maid cat who commands me
to feed her often, and to lavish love on her
when she deigns to permit.

Thanks for the humility
that inevitably comes from reflecting
on the myriads of reasons to be thankful for.
I am grateful for having consciously lived
and for the absence of desperate need
and for the time to reflect
on these great, good gifts.

Who or What are we thanking?
Does it matter? We don't actually have to know,
do we? Perhaps it's enough to recognize
that we do not make our way
entirely by our own desire; other *forces*—no
more explicit a distinction necessary—exist
on which we have little or no influence
but often profoundly influence us.
Let us remember to be grateful for these
breezes and gales bearing our inspirations
and here and there interpretations
of appreciation.

(Autumn 2005)

www.ingramcontent.com/pod-product-compliance
Lightning Source LLC
Chambersburg PA
CBHW031157020726

47499CB00002B/400